THE QUIET HAVEN

An Anthology of Readings on
Death and Heaven

Compiled by Ian Bradley

DARTON·LONGMAN+TODD

First published in 2021 by
Darton, Longman and Todd Ltd
1 Spencer Court
140 – 142 Wandsworth High Street
London SW18 4JJ

ISBN: 978-1-913657-30-7

A catalogue record for this book is available from the British Library.

Printed and bound in Great Britain by Bell & Bain, Glasgow

We sail the sea of life – a *Calm* One finds,
And One a *Tempest* – and, the voyage o'er,
Death is the quiet haven of us all.

William Wordsworth, 'Epitaph III', 1815

ACKNOWLEDGEMENTS

Sister Joyce Yarrow, the secretary for liturgy of the Society of St Francis, kindly allowed me to quote the prayer of commendation which appears in the prologue. Nicholas Ostler nobly translated the extract from the Brhadaranyaka Upanishad from the original Sanskrit, Dick Watson introduced me to De Witt Huntington's 'O think of the home over there' and John Winckler alerted me to the effect of A. J. Ayer's near-death experience. David Moloney and his colleagues at Darton, Longman & Todd have, as always, been immensely supportive of this project.

Contents

Preface

The inspiration for this book is both pastoral and personal. Over recent years I have found myself increasingly being asked about death and what may lie beyond it, often though not always by those themselves close to death or sensing that it cannot be far off. I felt the need to have a collection of suitable readings to hand, and it has grown into this anthology, compiled from the writings of some of the world's greatest minds and most devout believers over the last three thousand years.

I have had a long-standing interest in death and the afterlife, which goes back more than half a century to my teenage years. At the age of 16 I wrote a 'personal meditation on heaven', which included a poem I rather blush to read now. Alongside copious references to trumpets and angels, it contains the line 'calm yet lively, full yet striving', indicating a strong conviction that, as I put it, 'heaven is no feather bed; it must stretch our physical and mental powers to the full, keeping us active, healthy, sharp and keen. It is a place of excitement and rejoicing.' I did not realize then that I was echoing the thoughts of such eminent Christian preachers and thinkers as William Channing, F. D. Maurice and Benjamin Jowett (see extracts **34**, **42** and **57** in this anthology). I also quoted the High Lama's words about the Buddhist monastery of Shangri-La in James Hilton's novel *Lost Horizon*: 'Here you will achieve calmness and profundity, ripeness and wisdom and the clear enchantment of memory.'[1] Now that I have passed my three score years and ten, I am more drawn to the idea of heaven as a place of rest and calm – 'the quiet haven of us all', in William Wordsworth's words that give this book its title – although I still hope that there will also be activity and energy there.

This anthology includes poems and prayers which I have shared with those who have asked me about death and which I would wish to have read to me as I am dying as well as other passages suitable for more reflective reading. I hope it may serve as a useful and helpful resource for those who tend, counsel and minister to the sick, the anxious and the dying. I also hope that it will provide reassurance for those contemplating their own mortality, or the death of someone close to them. Several of the

---

[1]   James Hilton, *Lost Horizon* (London: Macmillan, 1933; quotation from London: Vintage, 2015), p. 138.

extracts offer a more detached theological or philosophical perspective and perhaps have more of an intellectual than a pastoral appeal. Maybe they will provide useful material for those groups which are increasingly meeting to reflect on and discuss the subject of death, as in the death cafés which have been set up in many parts of the world since the early 2010s.

The contents of the book are very varied. They range from brief epithets to longer poems and complex philosophical musings. Some are very simple and unashamedly sentimental, which may well be all that one can cope with as death approaches; others are more challenging and even disturbing. The overwhelming majority express a Christian perspective, but there are also extracts from the foundational texts of other faiths such as the Hindu Upanishads and from non-Christian mystics and philosophers. Every one of them is here because I have found it helpful, consoling or thought provoking in my own wrestling with what the great Spanish writer Federico García Lorca called the 'question beyond questions', the ultimately unfathomable mystery of death and what lies beyond it.

I have suggested on the page that follows this preface specific extracts which might be appropriate for particular situations and circumstances. This is in no way intended to be prescriptive, but it is designed to help swiftly identify, possibly in a crisis situation, something that may bring spiritual comfort and address specific concerns.

Together with prayers forming a prologue and epilogue and many shorter extracts embedded in the accompanying commentaries, there are sixty main readings in the anthology, arranged chronologically according to the date when they were written. Eleven come from ancient texts, including the Bible; seven are from medieval sources; fifteen are from the sixteenth, seventeenth and eighteenth centuries; twenty-five come from the nineteenth century; and two date from the early twentieth century.

It is no coincidence that the nineteenth century should provide so rich a source of material and the twentieth century furnish so little. The Victorian fascination/obsession with death is well known and well documented. It expressed itself in elaborate funerary and mourning rituals, death-bed scenes in novels, tear-jerkingly sentimental paintings and poems, children's hymns set in graveyards and agonized theological debate about the doctrine of eternal punishment. The Victorians took death extremely seriously and they talked and wrote about it openly and copiously. This was hardly surprising when it was an ever-present reality, nearly always occurring at home and often at a relatively young age. The average life expectancy of someone born in 1842, five years after Victoria's accession, was 40 for a boy and 42 for a girl. Today in the UK it is 79 and 83. In the earlier 1800s, over 17 per cent of infants died before their first birthday. Today's figure is 0.4%.

The twentieth century saw death being swept under the carpet and becoming a taboo subject to be avoided in conversation. Medical advances substantially cut mortality rates, put a premium on prolonging life at all costs and took death away from the home, shutting it off in the hospital side-ward. It was surely no coincidence that theologians largely ceased writing and thinking about heaven and the afterlife and concentrated instead on the here and now in what became known as 'realized eschatology'. As Bernhard Lang wrote in 2000:

> Twentieth-century theology has not been very kind to the notion of heaven as the abode of the blessed. Most theologians … describe heavenly existence in minimalist fashion … Some radical theologians have even gone as far as denying individual life after death altogether or are content with vague notions of individual human biographies being forever stored in God's eternal memory.[2]

The last decade or so has seen the beginnings of a significant change in attitude and approach. Doctors have begun to question the wisdom of trying to prolong life at all costs. In a much-reported series of BBC Reith lectures in 2014, Dr Atul Gawande, an American surgeon, highlighted our reluctance to recognize the limits of what medical practitioners can do and questioned modern medicine's emphasis on the quantity rather than quality of human life. Dame Sue Black, perhaps the world's best-known pathologist, has commended the Victorian approach and bemoaned the fact that Western culture has 'fallen out of love with death'.[3] Yet death is ceasing to be the last taboo. There are lively discussions around euthanasia (which properly means 'a good death' – at the right time and in the right way) and assisted dying. In 2011 Jon Underwood set up the first death café at his home in Hackney, London,

[2] Bernhard Lang, 'Heaven' in *The Oxford Companion to Christian Thought* (Oxford University Press, 2000), p. 288.
[3] Mike Wade, 'Dame Sue Black: There's Nothing Scary About Dead Bodies', *The Times*, 26 September 2020.

as a place where people, 'often strangers, could drink tea, eat cake and discuss death'.[4] There are now over 12,000 death cafés in 75 countries around the world. The coronavirus pandemic brought death to the forefront of news bulletins and the public consciousness and also led to a significant increase in the number of deaths taking place at home. We can no longer keep death at arm's length and out of sight.

Will this changing attitude lead to a greater interest in what lies beyond death? For most of human history, belief in some kind of immortality has been almost universal, shared by all the world's main faiths, civilizations and cultures. Writing at the dawn of the twentieth century, the anthropologist Sir James Frazer observed that 'the question whether our conscious personality survives after death has been answered by almost all races of men in the affirmative. On this point sceptical or agnostic peoples are nearly, if not wholly unknown.' Indeed, he went so far as to say that the idea of life after death 'must rank among the most firmly established of truths – were it out to the vote, it would command an overwhelming majority across humanity. The few dissenters would be overborne, their voices would be drowned in the general roar.'[5]

During the twentieth century, in parallel with the cover-up of death, belief in immortality began to falter, at least in the so-called developed, Western world. Elsewhere, it continued to be very widespread. George Orwell observed in 1944 that belief in survival after death 'is enormously less widespread than it was'.[6] It is true that there were some surprising converts to the idea. A. J. 'Freddie' Ayer, philosopher and one of the most prominent atheists of the twentieth century, noted that a near-death experience he had in 1988 when his heart stopped for four minutes 'provided rather strong evidence that death does not put an end to consciousness'. Like others, he returned from his brief 'death' a changed character – in the words of his wife, 'Freddie has got so much nicer since he died.'[7] But for the most part, particularly in the intellectual world, the conviction grew that this life is all that we have.

---

[4]   Any Cluett, 'The Death Cafe: A Medium Latte and a Chat About Dying', 29 January 2018, OUPblog (accessed 7 July 2021).
[5]   James Frazer, *The Belief in Immortality and the Worship of the Dead* Vol. 1 (London: Macmillan, 1913), p. 33.
[6]   George Orwell, *Seeing Things as They Are: Selected Journalism and Other Writings* (London: Penguin, 2016), p. 13.
[7]   Simon Critchley, *The Book of Dead Philosophers* (London: Granta, 2008), p. 262.

In Britain now, according to one recent poll, the balance is very evenly poised between believers and deniers. The UK Religion Survey undertaken in 2017 on behalf of the BBC found that the percentage of the population who believed in life after death was exactly the same as the percentage who did not – 46 per cent in each case – with just 8 per cent 'don't knows'. Belief in life after death seems to be significantly higher on the other side of the Atlantic, where a 2014 survey in the USA found that 72 per cent of respondents answered yes to the question 'Do you think there is life, or some sort of conscious existence, after death?'; 66 per cent of Canadians responded similarly in a 2018 poll. In Continental Europe, by contrast, it is significantly lower. Just 31 per cent of respondents in a 2018 survey in France said that they believed in life after death, as against 49 per cent who said that they did not, and 20 per cent who were unsure. Women consistently display more enthusiasm for the idea than men. Perhaps more surprisingly, in all these surveys belief in life beyond death is highest among millennials (those born between 1981 and 1996 and so in their 20s and 30s) and lowest among those over 65.

Maybe the fact that we have stopped burying our heads in the sand when it comes to thinking and talking about death means that there will be more interest and even belief in what comes after it. If so, then I hope this book will be timely and perhaps help to encourage this development.

Inevitably, thinking about the nature of post-mortem existence is a matter of conjecture and speculation. Some will say that it is idle and fruitless speculation born of mere pie-in-the-sky escapism and wish fulfilment. They will tend to agree with the response of Yama, the Hindu god of death, in the Katha Upanishad when, in the midst of a barrage of questions from a young boy, Nachiketas, he is asked whether humans continue or not to exist after death: 'It is a difficult and subtle matter. Choose another wish, Nachiketas, excuse me on this one and do not insist.'

But just because death is a mystery and we do not know what is in store for us beyond it, I do not think that means that we should not apply our God-given brains and imaginations to exploring the possibilities of the afterlife. It is not, after all, entirely a matter of idle speculation and conjecture. For those coming from a faith perspective, life beyond death is a clear promise that is made to us in our Scriptures, by God, and in the Christian understanding very specifically by Jesus both through his own death and resurrection and in his teaching. Christians approaching death believe that Jesus walked the path before them, accompanies

them on the journey and will be waiting to welcome them on the other
side. That said, there remain many imponderables, uncertainties and
questions, including, for the Christian, resurrection versus immorality,
universal versus limited salvation, and heaven or hell.

Every one of the extracts which follow, while acknowledging its real
pain and the grief that it brings in its wake, has an essentially positive
approach to death. Some enthusiastically court it and may appear rather
maudlin and morbid, although they accurately reflect the weariness
and readiness to die that it is undoubtedly often felt by those suffering
chronic and unbearable pain and by others towards the end of their
lives. Death is more than once described in the pages that follow as a
friend and even as a lover. In nearly every case, it is seen as an entirely
natural process, divinely ordained and part of the cycle of life, to be
embraced and welcomed in the same spirit as birth. Indeed, it is quite
often compared to birth, as it was by Martin Luther when he said in a
sermon on 'Preparing to Die' in 1519:

> Just as an infant is born with peril and pain from the small abode
> of its mother's womb into this immense heaven and earth, that is,
> into our world, so we depart this life through the narrow gate of
> death. And although the heavens and the earth in which we dwell
> at present seem large and wide to us, they are nevertheless much
> narrower and smaller than the mother's womb in comparison with
> the future heaven. Therefore, death is called a new birth.[8]

Perspectives on death are understandably conditioned by personality
and circumstances. Philosophers like Plato and Marcus Aurelius regard
it as a welcome liberation and disengagement from the 'confused crowd'
who inhabit this world and look forward to heaven as a place where
wisdom can truly be cultivated (**4** and **11**). For a chronic invalid like
Adelaide Anne Procter, 'the beautiful angel, Death' is to be welcomed
as one who will ease pain and 'soothe the terrors of thy troubled brain'
(**39** and **40**).

The extracts in this anthology envisage and describe death in all
sorts of ways – as a long and peaceful sleep leading to an eventual joyful
awakening, a journey, a pilgrimage, a homecoming and a reunion of

---

[8]   J. Pelikan and H. T. Lehman, *Luther's Works* (St Louis: Concordia; Philadelphia: For-
tress Press, 1955–1967), vol. 42 pp. 99–100.

friends who have been parted. Although notions of judgement, testing and purging are present, the overwhelming emphasis is on the ultimate destination and dwelling place for what Alfred Tennyson in his poem 'In Memoriam' calls 'the happy dead' as a heavenly paradise, a place of rest and joy. For some it is populated by white-clad angelic choirs, trees bearing a never-ending supply of succulent fruits and streets paved with gold, while for others it has more bracing qualities of the kind I commended in my adolescent poem or perhaps a simpler and more homely atmosphere.

The most recurrent and persistent imagining of death and the post-mortem existence in the pages that follow employs what one might call 'watery' metaphors of streams and rivers running down to the sea, droplets merging in a vast ocean, spray foam and waves, and of the individual human soul either crossing a river, setting out in a boat across the sea, or putting into a safe harbour or quiet haven, as in the lines by Wordsworth at the front of this book, or the closing couplet of the first verse of Charles Wesley's great hymn 'Jesu, Lover of My Soul':

> *Safe into thy haven guide,*
> *Oh receive my soul at last.*

It is certainly such images which most illuminate my own thinking about death, and my very inadequate attempts to give some kind of answer to those who ask me about it, whether they are anxious and troubled, or just plain curious. I am struck by the last words of the Orcadian poet George Mackay Brown before he died: 'I see hundreds and hundreds of ships sailing out of the harbour.'[9] For me, death is a great adventure and a journey not so much into the unknown as into the great ocean of God's love. Like rivers, streams, brooks and waterfalls, our lives find their destination in a divine embrace which is akin to the sea in its immensity, variety and combination of calm rest and ceaseless motion suggested by the ebb and flow of the tide and the rise and fall of the waves. By casting off and giving ourselves into that sea we find our quiet haven and much, much more besides. In the words of Psalm 23, God leads us to the water where we may rest, 'the quiet waters by' in the much-loved metrical version. I am conscious that this particular imagery for the afterlife, metaphorical as it is, does not sit easily with the passage

[9]   Ron Ferguson, *George Mackay Brown: The Wound and the Gift* (Edinburgh: St Andrew Press, 2011), p.363.

in the Book of Revelation on the new creation, which describes a new heaven and a new earth but 'no more sea' (**10**). This is consistent with the portrayal of the sea elsewhere in Revelation, and indeed throughout much of the Old Testament, as the remnant of the chaotic primordial state associated with evil and death. There are streams in the garden of the heavenly New Jerusalem, but there is no sea. In his hymn 'God Is the Refuge of His Saints', Isaac Watts contrasts the 'troubled ocean' and its fearful 'swelling tide' with the stream 'whose gentle flow makes glad the city of our God'. That reference in Revelation 21:1 is surely itself to be taken metaphorically rather than literally. George Matheson, several of whose biblical meditations appear in this anthology, certainly thought so. He felt that it alluded to the fact that in this life we are 'a multitude of little islands divided by stormy waves' whereas in the life to come 'the gulfs are all dried up' and human life becomes a connected continent.[10]

I suppose my own preferred metaphor for death does conform in some respects with another passage in the Book of Revelation (20:13), which describes the sea giving up its dead on the Day of Judgement to stand before God. Maybe that is indeed what will happen. But my vision is less apocalyptic and follows rather the teaching of the Upanishads, Rumi, John Scotus Eriugena, Christina Rossetti and others quoted in this anthology that our destiny is to return to and be embraced by the ocean of God's love. That is why this book has the title and the cover picture that it does, and it is why there are two passages among the many that follow that speak especially powerfully to me. The first is the extract from Kahlil Gibran's *The Prophet* (**60**), which begins with Almustafa saying 'I cannot tarry longer. The sea that calls all things unto her calls me, and I must embark.' It continues:

> He turned towards the sea, and saw his ship approaching the harbour, and upon her prow the mariners, the men of his own land. And his soul cried out to them, and he said: 'Sons of my ancient mother, you riders of the tides, how often have you sailed in my dreams and now you come in my awakening, which is my deeper dream. Ready am I to go, and my eagerness with sails full set awaits the wind. Only another breath will I breathe in this still air, only another loving look cast backward, and then I shall stand among you, a seafarer among seafarers.

---

[10] George Matheson, *Moments on the Mount: A Series of Devotional Meditations* (London: James Nisbet, 1884), p. 32.

And you, vast sea, sleepless mother, who alone are peace and freedom to the river and the stream, only another winding will this stream make, only another murmur in this glade, and then shall I come to you, a boundless drop to a boundless ocean.'[11]

The other much shorter extract that I would single out and which constitutes for me the single most powerful encapsulation of death and what lies beyond it is the verse penned by the blind George Matheson in his manse on the shore of the Firth of Clyde, the sound of whose waters had earlier prompted him to reflect 'Heaven somehow begins here, and immortality' (**53**):

> *O Love that wilt not let me go,*
> *I rest my weary soul in thee;*
> *I give thee back the life I owe,*
> *that in thine ocean depths its flow*
> *may richer, fuller be.*

---

[11]   Kahlil Gibran, *The Prophet* (London: William Heinemann, 1964), p.3

Suggested Extracts Which May Help in Particular Circumstances

For someone who is weary of life and ready to die: 21, 39, 40, 53

For someone who is frightened of death: 1, 9, 10, 23, 26, 29, 31, 39, 47, 52, Epilogue

For reading to someone close to death: Prologue, 1, 10, 16, 21, 22, 36, 43, 47, 49, 50, 52, 53, 55, Epilogue

For saying (or chanting) over the dying: Prologue, 10, 35, 49

For saying or reading just after someone has died: Prologue, 9, 12, 35, 44, 47, 48, 49, Epilogue

For use at a funeral: 1, 5, 6, 9, 10, 35, 38, 48

For someone who is asking questions about death: 15, 23, 25, 29, 30

For more philosophical and theological reflections about death and what lies beyond it: 2, 4, 7, 11, 13, 14, 18, 32, 34, 42, 54, 57

Longer passages suitable for meditation and quiet contemplation: 2, 20, 27, 28, 33, 37, 41, 45, 46, 51, 58, 59, 60

PROLOGUE
Two Prayers of Commendation

These two prayers of commendation, traditionally said either over the dying, at the end of a funeral service, or at a burial or committal in a crematorium, provide an appropriate introduction to this anthology.

The first clearly presents death as a journey, a theme which will recur in several of the extracts that follow and which is found in all the major faiths. In the funeral hymn of the Hindu Rig Veda, the departed soul is exhorted to 'go forth along the ancient pathways by which our ancestors have departed'. In addition to the Trinitarian God and the company of saints, it invokes angels – a key presence in many imaginings of the heavenly realm – and ends with the hope that the one who has died will find peace and a dwelling in the city of God.

In its original Latin form, beginning '*Proficiscere, anima Christiana, de hoc mundo*', this prayer goes back over a thousand years. In his book *Go Forth, Christian Soul: The Biography of a Prayer*,[12] John Lampard traces its origins to a Benedictine monastery in northern France or Germany in the late eighth century. The earliest-known text does not include the word 'Christian' before 'soul', giving it a more universal application. An early twelfth-century version from a monastery in Nursia, Italy, running to over seventy lines, makes much of the theme of setting the soul free.

The prayer largely disappeared from use in England from the time of the Reformation until John Henry Newman incorporated it into his 1865 poem *The Dream of Gerontius* (**45**). This led to its use in funeral liturgies as well as with the dying.

The second prayer similarly has a long pedigree, is found in many forms, and is widely used in funerals, burials and committals in crematoria. With its overarching sense of entrusting those who have died to God, who created us from the dust of the earth and to whom we will return, it asks Jesus as the Good Shepherd to look after his flock and forgive sins, and envisages heaven as the place where Christ will be seen face to face and the vision of God will delight for ever.

---

[12] John Lampard, *Go Forth, Christian Soul: The Biography of a Prayer* (Eugene, Oregon: Wipf & Stock, 2005), pp. xvi–xviii.

Go forth upon your journey from this world, O Christian soul, in the name of the Father who created you, in the name of the Son who suffered for you, in the name of the Holy Spirit who has called you out of darkness into glorious light. In communion with all the blessed saints and aided by the angels and archangels and all the heavenly host, may your portion this day be in peace and your dwelling in the city of God.

Our companion in faith and brother/sister in Christ, we entrust you to God who created you. May you return to the Most High who formed you from the dust of the earth. May the angels and the saints come to meet you as you go forth from this life. May Christ, who was crucified for you, take you into his Kingdom. May Christ the Good Shepherd give you a place within his flock. May Christ forgive you your sins and keep you among his people. May you see your Redeemer face to face and delight in the vision of God for ever.

1 Psalm 23
c. 1000–600 BCE

Possibly written as long ago as 1000 BCE, towards the end of the reign of King David, these verses constitute both the earliest and also almost certainly the most familiar of all the passages in this anthology.

In his book *Keeping Alive the Rumor of God*, which reflects theologically and pastorally on his forty years of parish ministry in the United Reformed Church, Martin Camroux writes, 'When I have visited the dying, I have usually found this is the most comforting text to have read to them, and often as I read it, they joined in.'[13] Psalm 23 is among the most frequently chosen Bible passages for funeral services, usually either being read in the Authorised Version or sung in the metrical version, both of which are given opposite.

The imagery is vivid and profoundly comforting. God is described as a shepherd, just as Jesus is in the New Testament, and as the one who makes us lie down in green pastures and leads us to or beside the quiet waters.

The reference to walking through the valley of the shadow of death can be taken either literally to describe our experience as we near the end of our earthly lives or metaphorically to indicate a state of depression, anxiety or danger. Either way, we are assured of God's comforting presence with us.

Similarly, the image of the table prepared for us can bear multiple meanings. In the context of death, it suggests the heavenly banquet at which we will feast with Christ, a prominent theme in early Christianity with its roots in Isaiah 25:6 and Matthew 8:11. The reference to the head being anointed with oil is suggestive of the sacrament of extreme unction practised in several branches of the Christian church in which those close to death are anointed with oil as part of the last rites.

The psalm ends with the author's confident affirmation 'I will dwell in the house of the Lord for ever'. Here is the promise of the quiet haven that awaits us after death, our heavenly home, described by Jesus in John 14:2: 'In my Father's house are many mansions ... I go to prepare a place for you' (**9**).

[13] Martin Camroux, *Keeping Alive the Rumor of God* (Eugene, Oregon: Wipf & Stock, 2020), p. 97.

The Lord is my shepherd; I shall not want.
He maketh me to lie down in green pastures: he leadeth me beside
the still waters.
He restoreth my soul: he leadeth me in the paths of righteousness for his
name's sake.
Yea, though I walk through the valley of the shadow of death, I will fear
no evil: for thou art with me; thy rod and thy staff they comfort me.
Thou preparest a table before me in the presence of mine enemies: thou
anointest my head with oil; my cup runneth over.
Surely goodness and mercy shall follow me all the days of my life: and I
will dwell in the house of the LORD for ever.

[1] The Lord's my shepherd, I'll not want.
He makes me down to lie
in pastures green; he leadeth me
the quiet waters by.
[2] My soul he doth restore again,
and me to walk doth make
within the paths of righteousness,
e'en for his own name's sake.
[3] Yea, though I walk in death's dark vale,
yet will I fear none ill,
for thou art with me and thy rod
and staff me comfort still.
[4] My table thou hast furnished
in presence of my foes.
My head thou dost with oil anoint,
and my cup overflows.
[5] Goodness and mercy all my life
shall surely follow me,
and in God's house forevermore
my dwelling place shall be.

2 THE BRHADARANYAKA UPANISHAD
c. 800–600 BCE

The earliest texts to wrestle deeply with the subject of death and what lies beyond it are the Upanishads, written in Sanskrit in the first millennium BCE and embodying the Vedic tradition at the heart of Hinduism.

Central to this tradition is the concept of Brahman, the ultimate reality and ground of all being, conceived as the creator and sustainer of the cosmos to which the soul (*atman*) of every individual will eventually return when it attains *moksha*, or liberation from rebirth.

The extracts opposite come from one of the oldest of the Upanishads and introduce several ideas about the afterlife, which resonate with aspects of later Judaeo-Christian belief. These include the conviction that a person on being born and assuming a bodily existence becomes acquainted with evil ('man is born to trouble as the sparks fly upwards', Job 5:7), but in dying leaves all that is wrong behind. There is also the close similarity between death and sleep ('those who sleep in the dust of the earth', Daniel 12:2), although in both Hinduism and Jewish–Christian tradition death transcends sleep and takes us to a realm beyond dreams. Loosened from the body, like a mango or fig being loosened from its stem, the soul returns to its source, breath, which remains as the immortal spirit. It is significant that in both Hebrew and Greek the same word (*ruach* and *pneuma* respectively) is used for both breath and spirit.

The Upanishads insist that the way to immortality lies through abandonment of the ego and all desires, prefiguring Jesus' words that 'whosoever will save his life shall lose it' (Matthew 16:25). The striking image at the end of this extract of the soul being turned into a new and more beautiful form, just as an embroideress fashions beautiful new patterns, seems to anticipate Paul's words about new spiritual bodies (**8**). Just as a snake sloughs off its old skin, so the dying person is freed from flesh and the pain that goes with it.

The later Katha Upanishad states: 'In heaven there is no fear. Death is not there and no one is afraid on account of old age. Leaving behind both hunger and thirst, and out of the reach of sorrow, all rejoice in the world of heaven.'

A person through being born and entering a body comes into contact with what is wrong but when he escapes from the body through dying he is cleansed of all wrong.

For the human being there are two dwelling places: here and in the other world; a third, which is in between, is the place of sleep. Standing in that twilight place, he sees both places, here and the other world. And when, with some effort, he attains the other world, he sees both what is bad and what is good and sleeps with his own brightness and his own light.

As a hawk or an eagle, tired of flying hither and yonder in the sky, folds its wings and holds a steady course to its nest, so the human spirit speeds to the state where it has no desires and no dreams. That state is beyond all desire and freed from ills and fears. Like a man in the embrace of a beloved woman, the one in the embrace of his sentient soul knows no without or within and has no desires or sorrows.

When the body falls into decline, whether through old age or sickness, like a fruit such as mango or a fig coming loose on its stalk, so the human soul, coming free of this body, retraces its path to its source, breath itself. When this soul falls as into a faint, then the breaths are drawn in and the sources of energy are concentrated on the heart. The top of the heart shines forth, and through this shining the soul escapes, through eye or head or some other part of the body. The breath follows on close behind and as it escapes, so the person becomes clear-sighted, his knowledge, his deeds and his past experience possessing him.

Just as an embroideress, taking the measure of an outline, fashions it in another form, newer and more beautiful, so this self, shaking off its body and dismissing ignorance, creates another newer and more beautiful form.

With the loss of desire does the mortal become immortal and attain Brahman. As a dead snake's skin lies abandoned on an ant-hill, just so does the body lie. As for the breath, bodiless but immortal, it is Brahman and energy.

3 THE MUNDAKA UPANISHAD
c. 400–200 BCE

The quotation opposite introduces one of the most common ways in which the journey of the soul through death has been imagined by using the analogy of a river running into the sea.

This idea is especially associated with the Eastern religions of Hinduism and Buddhism. Another of the later Upanishads (Prashna), which scholars think may display Buddhist influences, ends similarly by evoking the image of flowing rivers ultimately losing their name and shape and being simply called the ocean. Other Upanishads describe the universe at its beginning as consisting just of water and even suggest that Brahman is a product of this primeval sea, so a return to Brahman is almost literally a return to the ocean. Similar language is found in the *Tao Te Ching*, the foundational text of the Chinese religion and philosophy of Taoism: 'To Tao all under heaven will come as streams and torrents flow into a great river or sea.'

Christians, too, have often used the analogy of rivers flowing into the sea to describe death and what lies beyond it. It is directly invoked in Christina Rossetti's poems (47). The twentieth-century American mystic Thomas Merton wrote of 'the rivers of tranquillity which flow from God, out into the whole universe and draw all things back to God'.[14] Perhaps the fullest Christian expression of this idea is found in the writings of the German Dominican mystic Meister Eckhart (c. 1260–c. 1328):

> When I go back into the ground, into the depths, into the well-spring of the Godhead, no one will ask me whence I came or whither I went … Henceforth one cannot speak about the soul any more, for she has lost her name yonder in the oneness of divine essence. There she is no more called soul; she is called infinite being. She plunges into the bottomless well of the divine nature and becomes one with God.

Eckhart seems to echo the Upanishads in suggesting that in death individual identity disappears, becoming absorbed into the divine essence. There has been much debate about this in both the Hindu Vedic tradition and Christian thinking.

---

[14] Thomas Merton, *Seeds of Contemplation* (Norfolk, Connecticut: New Directions, 1949), p. 180.

As the flowing rivers disappear in the sea, losing their name and their form, thus a wise man, freed from name and form, goes to the divine person, who is greater than the great.

4 PLATO, *PHAEDO*
c. 360 BCE

The Greek philosopher Plato (c. 427–c. 347 BCE) produced more comprehensive arguments for the immortality of the soul than anyone else in the ancient world. They have been hugely influential, not least in Christian thinking.

The case for continuing existence beyond death is made most persuasively in his dialogue *Phaedo*, in which he used his teacher and mentor Socrates to express his own ideas. In his last hours before facing death by poisoning at the hands of the Athenian state, as happened in 399 BCE, Socrates is portrayed as being in discussion with his students, one of whom, Phaedo, records their conversation.

Like the authors of the Upanishads, Plato sees the soul as existing before birth and after death, and thus having both a former and a future life. Being in the image and likeness of the divine, it is immortal, unchangeable and indissoluble, whereas the body, being in the image and likeness of the human, is mortal, changeable and corruptible. Death, which involves the separation of the soul from the body, is something to be welcomed, particularly by a philosopher, as it frees one from the distractions that come from bodily pleasures and senses as well as from the corruption and evil of this world. In Plato's words:

> That soul, herself invisible, departs to the invisible world, to the divine and immortal and rational: thither arriving, she lives in bliss and is released from the error and folly of men, their fears and wild passions and all other human ills, and forever dwells in company with the gods.

Plato has Socrates, as a philosopher seeking wisdom, welcoming and embracing death just as the swans do with their singing. Others, he suggests, will have somewhat different experiences of the afterlife, depending on their attitudes and behaviour in this life. He envisages an element of judgement and portrays the dead as being gathered together in various regions under and above the earth, with the irredeemably wicked being destined for the deep underground pit of Tartarus while other sinners undergo a kind of temporary purgatory in the river Acheron, from which they will emerge to join purer and more enlightened souls.

There is great reason to hope that, going whither I go, when I have come to the end of my journey, I shall attain that which has been the pursuit of my life. And therefore I go on my way rejoicing, and not I only, but every other man who believes that his mind has been made ready and that he is in a manner purified.

What is purification but the separation of the soul from the body, the habit of the soul gathering and collecting herself into herself and dwelling in her own place? This separation and release of the soul from the body is termed death.

The true philosophers are ever seeking to release the soul. Is not the separation and release of the soul from the body their especial study? The true philosophers are always occupied in the practice of dying, wherefore also to them least of all men is death terrible. Look at the matter thus: if they have been in every way the enemies of the body, and are wanting to be alone with the soul, when this desire of theirs is granted, how inconsistent would they be if they trembled and repined, instead of rejoicing at their departure to that place where, when they arrive, they hope to gain that which in life they desired – wisdom. Many a man has been willing to go to the world beyond animated by the hope of seeing there an earthly love, or wife, or son, and conversing with them. And will he who is a true lover of wisdom, and is strongly persuaded that only in the world beyond he can worthily enjoy her, still repine at death? Will he not depart with joy? Surely he will if he be a true philosopher. For he will have a firm conviction that there and there only, he can find wisdom in her purity. And if this be true, he would be very absurd if he were afraid of death.

Will you not allow that I have as much of the spirit of prophecy in me as the swans? For they, when they perceive that they must die, having sung all their life long, do then sing more than ever, rejoicing in the thought that they are about to go away to the god whose ministers they are.

5 THE BOOK OF ECCLESIASTES
c. 330–250 BCE

The so-called Wisdom books in the Old Testament provide the first significant treatment of death and what follows it to be found in the Bible. It is appropriately tentative and tantalizingly brief but sets out several themes taken up in Christian thought.

The overall emphasis in the Book of Ecclesiastes, which draws much on the prevailing wisdom traditions in the ancient Near East, is on the transitory, illusory and even futile nature of all things in this world, as expressed in the famous phrase 'Vanity of vanities; all is vanity' (1:2). Alongside this somewhat depressing view, however, there is an underlying emphasis on the basic rhythm of the cycle of life and both the inevitability and the naturalness of death. This is memorably stated in the first quotation opposite, which reminds us that there is a time and season for everything, not least a time to be born and a time to die.

Death awaits all creatures and in facing it, humans are no different from and have no advantages over animals. All have come from dust and all will return to dust again. This observation directly echoes the words said by God to Adam in the garden of Eden as recorded in Genesis 3:19: 'dust you are and to dust you will return'.

Yet although this may be the fate of the physical body after death, it is not the whole story. Humans go to their eternal home and just as the dust returns to the earth from which it came, the spirit returns to God who gave and created it.

The author of the Book of Ecclesiastes does not minimize the pain, dislocation and finality of death – indeed, in speaking of the silver cord being snapped and the pitcher broken, he uses some of the most graphic imagery in the Bible to describe it. Nor does he offer any easy and glib answers to the question of what happens after death. But while acknowledging that it is a mystery about which there is no point in us enquiring or fretting too much, he is clear that it involves both a homecoming and a return to God.

For everything there is a season, and a time for every matter under heaven: a time to be born, and a time to die.

3:1–2

The fate of the sons of men and the fate of beasts is the same; as one dies, so dies the other. They all have the same breath, and man has no advantage over the beasts; for all is vanity. All go to one place; all are from the dust, and all turn to dust again. Who knows whether the spirit of man goes upward and the spirit of the beast goes down to the earth? So I saw that there is nothing better than that a man should enjoy his work, for that is his lot; who can bring him to see what will be after him?

3:19–22

All must go to their eternal home, and the mourners go about the streets before the silver cord is snapped, and the golden bowl is broken, and the pitcher is broken at the fountain, and the wheel broken at the cistern, and the dust returns to the earth as it was, and the spirit returns to God who gave it.

12:5–7
(New Revised Standard Version)

6 THE WISDOM OF SOLOMON
c.50 BCE

O f the books that make up the Christian Old Testament and Apocrypha and the Septuagint, the Wisdom of Solomon was the last to be written. It draws heavily on Plato's distinction between the body and the soul and on his doctrine of immortality. It also introduces an idea that was to become very powerful in later Christian thinking – that death was not part of God's original plan and intention for humanity but was brought into the world through the devil and those who followed him in turning their back on God and doing evil.

This idea is foreshadowed in God's curse in Genesis 3:19, when Adam is told that because he has eaten from the forbidden tree 'dust you are, and to dust you will return', but the link between death and human sin, prompted by the devil, is made much more explicit in the passage opposite. It seems to contradict what Ecclesiastes says about the naturalness and inevitability of death in the cycle of existence. These two radically different views of death – as a natural, almost God-given process or as an affront to God's purposes brought about by the workings of the devil and through human sinfulness – have continued to co-exist in uneasy tension in Christian thought.

The Wisdom of Solomon also clearly states that while the souls of the righteous and faithful will enjoy unending happiness with God, the wicked and godless will receive punishment. There is an unmistakable note of judgement and an emphatic indication that the post-mortem state for each individual will depend on how he or she has lived in this life.

By this stage, the notion of bodily resurrection after death had come into Jewish thought. It is clearly there in the Book of Daniel, which pre-dates the Wisdom of Solomon by over a hundred years, and where it is stated that 'many of those who sleep in the dust of the earth shall awake, some to everlasting life, and some to shame and everlasting contempt' (Dan. 12:2). The Wisdom of Solomon makes no allusion to bodily resurrection, although it seems to admit the possibility of the resurrection of bodies in spiritualized form.

God created man to be immortal, and made him to be an image of his own eternity. Nevertheless through envy of the devil came death into the world: and they that do hold of his side do find it.

But the souls of the righteous are in the hand of God, and there shall no torment touch them. In the sight of the unwise they seemed to die: and their departure is taken for misery, and their going from us to be utter destruction: but they are in peace. For though they be punished in the sight of men, yet is their hope full of immortality. And having been a little chastised, they shall be greatly rewarded: for God proved them, and found them worthy for himself. As gold in the furnace hath he tried them, and received them as a burnt offering. And in the time of their visitation they shall shine, and run to and fro like sparks among the stubble.

2:23–3:7

(Authorised [King James] Version)

7 CICERO, *DE SENECTUTE*
44 BCE

The Roman statesman Marcus Tullius Cicero (106–43 BCE) wrote his treatise on old age when he was 63, although he presented it as a discourse delivered by Marcus Portius Cato , a senator known as Cato the Elder, in his 84th year.

Shortly after writing *De Senectute* (*On Old Age*), Cicero was put to death as an enemy of the state because of his opposition to the three-man dictatorship which ruled the Roman Republic after the death of Julius Caesar.

Strongly influenced by Plato's doctrine of the immortality of the soul, Cicero presents the body as a prison from which the soul is liberated and purified by death. He is one of the first writers that I can discover to employ the reassuring image of death as being like seeing land and entering the harbour after a long voyage across an ocean.

He also makes the analogy first found in the Upanishads between death and sleep, suggesting that it is when sleeping that souls most clearly show their divine origin and nature and also that through dreaming they see most clearly into the future and the afterlife. Shakespeare's words given to Hamlet in his famous soliloquy 'To be, or not to be?'[15] come to mind:

> To die, to sleep.
> To sleep, perchance to dream – ay, there's the rub.
> For in that sleep of death what dreams may come
> When we have shuffled off this mortal coil.[16]

Particularly striking is Cicero's closing observation that we leave life as from an inn rather than a home, 'for nature has given us here a lodging for sojourn, not a place of habitation'. A similar sense is found in Christianity, as classically expressed in the Epistle to the Hebrews 13:14: 'Here we have no abiding city, but we are looking for the city that is to come.' The seventh-century Irish monk Columbanus wrote 'since we are travellers and pilgrims in this world, let us think of the end of the road, that is of our life, for the end of our way is our home'.

---

[15] Act 3 Scene 1 line 57.
[16] Act 3 Scene 1, lines 65–69.

This ripeness of old age is to me so pleasant, that, in proportion as I draw near to death, I seem to see land, and after a long voyage to be on the point of entering the harbour.

While we are shut up in this prison of the body, we are performing a heavy task laid upon us by necessity; for the soul, of celestial birth, is forced down from its supremely high abode, and plunged into the earth, a place uncongenial with its divine nature and its eternity. I believe that the gods disseminated souls, and planted them in human bodies, that there might be those who should hold the earth in charge, and contemplating the order of celestial beings, should copy it in symmetry and harmony of life. As the soul is always active, so it can have no end of motion; moreover, since the nature of the soul is uncompounded, it is indivisible and imperishable.

Indeed, I never could be persuaded that souls live while they are in mortal bodies and die when they depart from them, nor yet that the soul becomes void of wisdom on leaving a senseless body; but I have believed that when, freed from all corporeal mixture, it begins to be pure and entire, it then is wise. Moreover, when the constitution of man is dissolved by death, it is obvious what becomes of each of the other parts; for they all go whence they came: but the soul alone is invisible, alike when it is present in the body and when it departs.

You see nothing so nearly resembling death as sleep. Now in sleep souls most clearly show their divineness; for when they are thus relaxed and free, they foresee the future. From this we may understand what they will be when they have entirely released themselves from the bonds of the body.

I depart from life, as from an inn, not as from a home; for nature has given us here a lodging for a sojourn, not a place of habitation. O glorious day, when I shall go to that divine company and assembly of souls, and when I shall depart from this crowd and tumult!

8 PAUL'S FIRST LETTER TO THE CORINTHIANS

c. 53–57 CE

Belief in bodily resurrection after death was widespread in Judaism by the time of Jesus and was particularly strongly held by the Pharisees. It was generally seen as something that did not happen immediately post-mortem but following an intermediate state akin to sleeping.

Jesus' followers took up this idea after his death, linking it to his own resurrection from the tomb, which they saw as vanquishing death and opening the way to eternal life for all believers.

St Paul, whose own encounter with the risen Jesus while on the way to Damascus is recorded three times in the Book of Acts, was the prime architect and exponent of the doctrine of resurrection, which came to be a central tenet of Christian teaching and understanding about death and what lies beyond it, as expressed in the affirmation at the end of the Apostles' Creed: 'I believe in the resurrection of the body and in life everlasting.'

The extract from Paul's writings which is printed opposite and often read at funerals provides the fullest exposition in the Bible of this doctrine and one of the most significant biblical treatments of life after death. While densely written and not always easy to understand, it clearly rests the Christian's hope of eternal life on Jesus' rising from the dead as the second or last Adam, breaking the curse of death pronounced on the first Adam. In the words of the New Testament scholar Tom Wright in his book *The Resurrection of the Son of God*, this hope consists 'not in going on and on for ever, not in an endless cycle of death and rebirth, not in a blessed disembodied mortal existence, but in a newly embodied life, a transformed physicality'.[17]

Mention of the last trumpet at the end of this passage reflects Paul's expectation of an apocalyptic end time when Christ will return, ushering in a general resurrection when the Christian dead will rise from their sleep and those still alive 'shall be caught up together with them in the clouds, to meet the Lord in the air: and so shall we ever be with the Lord' (1 Thessalonians 4:17, New International Version).

[17] Tom Wright, *The Resurrection of the Son of God* (London: SPCK, 2003), p.682

Someone will ask, 'How are the dead raised? With what kind of body do they come?' You foolish man! What you sow does not come to life unless it dies. And what you sow is not the body which is to be, but a bare kernel, perhaps of wheat or of some other grain. But God gives it a body as he has chosen, and to each kind of seed its own body. For not all flesh is alike, but there is one kind for men, another for animals, another for birds, and another for fish. There are celestial bodies and there are terrestrial bodies ...

So is it with the resurrection of the dead. What is sown is perishable, what is raised is imperishable. It is sown in dishonour, it is raised in glory. It is sown in weakness, it is raised in power. It is sown a physical body, it is raised a spiritual body. If there is a physical body, there is also a spiritual body. Thus it is written, 'The first man Adam became a living being'; the last Adam became a life-giving spirit. But it is not the spiritual which is first but the physical, and then the spiritual. The first man was from the earth, a man of dust; the second man is from heaven. As was the man of dust, so are those who are of the dust; and as is the man of heaven, so are those who are of heaven. Just as we have borne the image of the man of dust, we shall also bear the image of the man of heaven ...

Lo! I tell you a mystery. We shall not all sleep, but we shall all be changed, in a moment, in the twinkling of an eye, at the last trumpet. For the trumpet will sound, and the dead will be raised imperishable, and we shall be changed. For this perishable nature must put on the imperishable, and this mortal nature must put on immortality. Then shall come to pass the saying that is written: 'Death is swallowed up in victory. O death, where is thy victory? O death, where is thy sting?'

15:35–55
(Revised Standard Version)

9 ST JOHN'S GOSPEL
c. 70–100 CE

As reported and quoted in the gospels, Jesus himself says relatively little about death and what lies beyond it. Aside from his comment 'I am the resurrection and the life. Anyone who believes in me will live, even after dying' (John 11:25), he does not mention the idea of the resurrection of the dead.

Indeed, in contrast to the doctrine promulgated by Paul of a general resurrection at the end of time, in which the righteous dead will arise from an intermediate state of sleep, Jesus seems rather to hold to the view that the dead ascend directly to heaven, as suggested in his comment to the thief who is crucified next to him: 'today you will be with me in paradise' (Luke 23:43).

Most of what Jesus does say about the afterlife is found in St John's Gospel. The first of the quotations opposite, about the necessity of the grain of wheat being buried in the ground and dying if it is to bear fruit, speaks powerfully of life coming out of death.

The middle extract, containing the familiar verses in which Jesus talks about there being many mansions in his Father's house, constitutes perhaps the most quoted of all Bible passages in funeral and cremation services. As well as suggesting that there is a broad and varied dimension to heaven, the emphasis here is on Jesus going there to prepare a place for us and on his coming again to receive us and welcome us there, so that where he is, we may be also.

This passage ends with a deep expression of peace and reassurance in which he tells us that we should not be troubled or afraid in the face of death. That message is repeated in the last extract opposite in which Jesus promises that he will see us again and that our sorrow will be turned to rejoicing of a kind that no one can take away from us.

Verily, verily, I say unto you, Except a corn of wheat fall into the ground
and die, it abideth alone: but if it die, it bringeth forth much fruit.

12:24

Let not your heart be troubled: ye believe in God, believe also in me.
In my Father's house are many mansions: if it were not so, I would
have told you. I go to prepare a place for you.
And if I go and prepare a place for you, I will come again, and receive
you unto myself; that where I am, there ye may be also.
Peace I leave with you, my peace I give unto you: not as the world giveth,
give I unto you. Let not your heart be troubled, neither let it be
afraid.

14:1–3, 27

Ye now have sorrow: but I will see you again, and your heart shall
rejoice,
and your joy no man taketh from you.

16:22

(Authorised [King James] version)

10 The Revelation to John
c. 96 CE

The apocalyptic Book of Revelation, which was probably written by a Christian from Ephesus known as 'John the Elder' while on the island of Patmos, either as an exile or on a preaching tour, provides the Bible's fullest and most detailed description of heaven conceived of as a new creation at the end of time. Significantly, it is a new heaven which emerges, together with a new earth in the form of a holy city or new Jerusalem, sent down by God.

The emphasis here is on a place where God is present and from which pain, sorrow and death have been banished. This reassuring message is confirmed in another much-quoted verse from Revelation 14:13: 'I heard a voice from heaven saying unto me, "Write, Blessed are the dead which die in the Lord from henceforth": "Yea", saith the Spirit, "that they may rest from their labours; and their works do follow them."' Other verses describe heaven as being filled with white-robed angels continually singing and worshipping God.

The second extract opposite gives a physical description of paradise which has been hugely influential in Christian imaginings of the heavenly state (see **15, 22, 29** and **43**). The striking imagery of a river and trees bearing all kinds of fruits is not just found in Christianity. The Quran paints a similar picture when describing the post-mortem existence of devout Muslims: 'They shall have gardens beneath which rivers flow to abide in them for ever ... the gardens of perpetual abode which they will enter along with those who do good from among their parents and their spouses and their offspring; and the angels will enter in upon them from every gate.' Like Christianity, Islam envisages a day of judgement in which the souls of the evil and the good will be separated, with the righteous and faithful undergoing resurrection and living for ever in a perfect and beautiful place.

Both Christians and Muslims have designed gardens to represent paradise. Perhaps the most impressive are those in the Alhambra in Granada, Spain, where streams of water flow through flower beds and orchards. Medieval monastic cloister gardens were often similarly designed with a fountain in the centre, symbolizing Christ as the water of life.

And I saw a new heaven and a new earth: for the first heaven and the first earth were passed away; and there was no more sea.

And I John saw the holy city, new Jerusalem, coming down from God out of heaven, prepared as a bride adorned for her husband.

And I heard a great voice out of heaven saying, Behold, the tabernacle of God is with men, and he will dwell with them, and they shall be his people, and God himself shall be with them, and be their God.

And God shall wipe away all tears from their eyes; and there shall be no more death, neither sorrow, nor crying, neither shall there be any more pain: for the former things are passed away.

And he that sat upon the throne said, Behold, I make all things new.

And he said unto me, Write: for these words are true and faithful.

And he said unto me, It is done. I am Alpha and Omega, the beginning and the end. I will give unto him that is athirst of the fountain of the water of life freely.

21:1-6

And he shewed me a pure river of water of life, clear as crystal, proceeding out of the throne of God and of the Lamb.

In the midst of the street of it, and on either side of the river, was there the tree of life, which bare twelve manner of fruits, and yielded her fruit every month: and the leaves of the tree were for the healing of the nations.

And there shall be no more curse: but the throne of God and of the Lamb shall be in it; and his servants shall serve him:

And they shall see his face; and his name shall be in their foreheads.

And there shall be no night there; and they need no candle, neither light of the sun; for the Lord God giveth them light: and they shall reign for ever and ever.

22:1-5

(Authorised [King James] Version)

11 MARCUS AURELIUS, MEDITATIONS
c. 170–180 CE

Marcus Aurelius, Roman Emperor from 161 to 180 BCE, was a leading exponent of Stoicism, the Hellenistic school of philosophy known for its rationalism, love of moderation and calm resilience. For him, death is an entirely natural occurrence, which he compares to a woman giving birth, and not to be feared or dreaded in any way. It heralds either an extinction of the senses or the acquiring of a different set of sensations.

Whatever it leads to, there is much to welcome in the release from the 'impulses of the appetites and the passions, the toilsome reasonings and the servitude to the flesh' that death brings. Like Plato, Marcus Aurelius approaches death as a philosopher seeking wisdom and clarity and only too keen to leave the confusion and muddle of life. The Grand Inquisitor's observation in *The Gondoliers* (**56**) about death being the only true unraveller of life's closely complicated tangle come to mind.

Another meditation by Marcus Aurelius underlines his view of death as a great equalizer as well as a great unraveller: 'Alexander the Great and his mule driver both died and the same thing happened to both. They were absorbed alike into the life force of the world, or dissolved alike into atoms.' He also adhered to a belief in the regenerative cycle of life and death in the physical world, approvingly quoting the Greek philosopher Heraclitus' observation that 'the death of earth is the birth of water, the death of water is the birth of atmosphere, the death of atmosphere is fire'.

What gives Marcus Aurelius a place in this anthology is not his philosophical musings, interesting as they are, but the calm and cheerful manner in which he approaches death as a wholly natural occurrence. It is, he observes, the nature of all things to change, turn and corrupt, so that others may spring out of them. 'Depart, therefore, contented, and in good humour.'

Death is, like our birth, a mystery of nature; the one a commixture of elements, the other a resolution into them: In neither is there anything shameful, or unsuitable to the intellectual nature, or contrary to the intention of its structure.

Death is the cessation of the sensual impressions, of the impulses of the appetites and passions, of the toilsome reasonings, and of the servitude to the flesh. He who dreads death dreads either an extinction of all sense, or dreads a different sort of sensation. If all sense is extinguished, there can be no sense of evil. If a different sort of sense is acquired, you become another sort of living creature; and don't cease to live.

Don't despise death; but receive it well-pleased, as it is one of the things which nature wills. For such as it is to be young, to be old, to grow up, to be full grown; to breed teeth, and beard, and grow grey; to beget, to go with child, to be delivered; and undergo the other natural effects which the seasons of your life produce; such is it also to be dissolved. It becomes a man of wisdom neither to be inconsiderate, impetuous, or ostentatiously contemptuous about death; but await the season of it, as of one of the operations of nature. As you are now awaiting the season when the foetus shall come out of the womb of your wife, thus await the season when your soul shall fall out of these its teguments [the enveloping membrane of the body]. If you want also a popular support, here is one which goes to the heart: you will be extremely easy with regard to death, if you consider the objects you are going to leave; and the manners of that confused crowd from which you are to be disengaged.

Yet a little, and you shall be no more; nor shall any of those things remain, which you now behold; nor any of those who are now living. 'Tis the nature of all things to change, to turn, and to corrupt; that others may, in their course, spring out of them.

Depart, therefore, contented, and in good humour.

12 ADOMNÁN'S DESCRIPTION OF THE DEATH OF ST COLUMBA
c. 697–700

The moving description quoted opposite from the *Life of Columba* written by Adomnán describes the saint's death in the small monastic chapel on the Scottish island of Iona in 597. Although it focuses rather more on the moment of death than on what lies beyond, I have included it in this anthology because of its depiction of the journey into the next world and the role played by angels in facilitating it. It has a special significance for me as the church in which I was baptized, at Toward on the Cowal peninsula in Argyll, has a stained-glass window showing Columba at his moment of death, his eyes gazing towards heaven from where two angels have descended to meet him.

The image of angels coming down from heaven to meet departing souls and escort them on their own journey there recurs throughout Christian literature and art. It is particularly prominent in later accounts of the deaths of Celtic saints. The *Life of Ninian*, written by Ailred of Rievaulx in the mid-twelfth century, portrays the saint associated with the early monastery of Whithorn in south-west Scotland being surrounded by a shining host, 'blazing bright in snow-white vestment' and carried in angel arms 'beyond the stars of heaven'. Once there, his soul passes through the company of saints and more angelic hosts and comes into the presence of the King enthroned on high, joining in hymns of gladness glorifying the Trinity. The *Book of the Anchorite of Llanddewibrefi*, dating from 1356, describes the soul of the Welsh saint David being borne by angels to a place of rest without labour, joy without sadness, health without sickness and youth and vigour without old age, where Christ's champions are commended and the undeserving wealthy are ignored.

Adomnán's account of Columba's journey through death focuses almost entirely on the role and presence of the angels who surround him and on the brilliant light and the sweet sound of singing which accompanies them as they bear him aloft. His remark that the saint's face after death had the appearance 'of one alive and sleeping' suggests passage into an intermediate state of sleep before the last judgement and resurrection.

The saint, as we have been told by some who were present, even before his soul departed, opened wide his eyes and looked round him from side to side, with a countenance full of wonderful joy and gladness, no doubt seeing the holy angels coming to meet him. Diarmit [Columba's servant] then raised the holy right hand of the saint, that he might bless his assembled monks. And the venerable father himself moved his hand at the same time, as well as he was able, that, as he could not in words while his soul was departing, he might at least, by the motion of his hand, be seen to bless his brethren. And having given them his holy benediction in this way, he immediately breathed his last. After his soul had left the tabernacle of the body, his face still continued ruddy, and brightened in a wonderful way by his vision of the angels, and that to such a degree that he had the appearance not so much of one dead, as of one alive and sleeping.

I must not omit to mention the revelation made to a certain saint of Ireland, at the very time the blessed soul departed. A holy man named Lugud, one who had grown old in the service of Christ, and was noted for his sanctity and wisdom, had a vision which at early dawn he told to one called Fergnous, who was like himself a servant of Christ. 'In the middle of this last night,' said he, 'Columba, the pillar of many churches, passed to the Lord; and at the moment of his blessed departure, I saw in the spirit the whole island of Iona, where I never was in the body, resplendent with the brightness of angels; and the whole heavens above it, up to the very zenith, were illumined with the brilliant light of the same heavenly messengers, who descended in countless numbers to bear away his holy soul. At the same moment, also, I heard the loud hymns and entrancingly sweet canticles of the angelic host, as his holy soul was borne aloft amidst the ascending choirs of angels.'

13 THE VENERABLE BEDE ON A SPARROW FLYING THROUGH A HOUSE
731

In this passage from his *Ecclesiastical History of the English People*, written while he was a monk in Jarrow, Tyneside, in north-east England, the Venerable Bede gives a rather beautiful picture of the brevity of human life and the mystery of what precedes and follows it by making the comparison with a bird flying in and out of a warm hall in the midst of a winter storm.

Bede puts this analogy into the mouth of one of the chief courtiers of Edwin, the early seventh-century Northumbrian king, at a time when he was seriously considering converting to the Christian faith already espoused by his wife, Aethelburh, a Kentish princess, and being preached in his kingdom by the missionary bishop Paulinus. The chief specifically commends the new faith to his royal master because of the light that it shines and the hope that it offers in respect of what happens after death.

Edwin did, indeed, convert to Christianity and was baptized by Paulinus in York in 627. Paulinus went on to convert large numbers of Edwin's subjects, baptizing them in the river Glen at Yeavering, on the edge of the Cheviot hills in north Northumberland.

A somewhat similar image to illustrate the mystery of death is used by Henry Vaughan in his poem 'Dear, Beauteous Death' (**27**) when he points out that we do not know where the bird who has fled its nest has gone. The brevity of this life and the joys and rest of the eternal life to come are well captured in verses by Bernard of Cluny, translated by John Mason Neale:

> *Brief life is here our portion,*
> *Brief sorrow, short-lived care;*
> *The life that knows no ending,*
> *The tearless life is there.*
> *O happy retribution,*
> *Short toil, eternal rest;*
> *For mortals and for sinners*
> *A mansion with the blest.*

The present life of man upon earth seems to me, in comparison with that time which is unknown to us, like to the swift flight of a sparrow through the house wherein you sit at supper in winter, with your ealdormen and thegns, while the fire blazes in the midst, and the hall is warmed, but the wintry storms of rain or snow are raging abroad. The sparrow, flying in at one door and immediately out at another, whilst he is within is safe from the wintry tempest; but after a short space of fair weather, he immediately vanishes out of your sight, passing from winter into winter again. So this life of man appears for a little while, but of what is to follow or what went before we know nothing at all. If, therefore, this new doctrine tells us something more certain, it seems justly to deserve to be followed.

14 JOHN SCOTUS ERIUGENA ON THE INEFFABLE RETURN
c. 866

I have chosen this somewhat dense philosophical reflection because of its message that all created things, including humans, will return to God, from whom they have originally come. This theme of 'an ineffable return', which is repeated in several passages in this anthology, finds its most emphatic expression in John Scotus Eriugena's lengthy work *Periphyseon*.

Eriugena (c. 800–c. 877), who was born and educated in Ireland but spent most of his adult life in France, is widely regarded as the outstanding European theologian and philosopher of the early Middle Ages. Deeply influenced by early Greek theologians in the neo-Platonic tradition, like Maximus the Confessor, who is quoted opposite, he espoused an essentially universalist position, holding that all souls will be saved and held in the embrace of divine love. He suggested that rather than being created by God from nothing, as traditional orthodox Christian doctrine maintained, all creatures proceed or emanate from God's very being and eventually return there. Creation is an unfolding as well as a manifestation of the unfathomable divine nature, into which it will ultimately be re-absorbed. Corporeal beings will return to their incorporeal first cause, the temporal to the eternal, and the finite to the infinite, with the human mind achieving reunification with the divine mind.

For Eriugena, our conversion into God is like the transmutation of air into light, and as we are absorbed back into the divine we become overshadowed just as stars do when the sun rises. Difficult as his philosophy is to grasp, it is grounded in the overriding conviction that God is all in all, that love is the basis of everything and that every human soul will attain the eternal life that comes from re-absorption into the mind and love of God from which we first came.

Later Christian writers have expressed this idea more simply. The Victorian Jesuit priest and poet Gerard Manley Hopkins began a poem 'Thee, God, I come from, to Thee go'. When the twentieth-century Welsh poet and Anglican priest R. S. Thomas was asked how he felt about death, he replied, 'We came from God and go to God. That is good enough for me.' For the Swiss Catholic theologian Hans Küng, death was 'a passing into God.'

Maximus the Confessor teaches that the cause of all things is the end of all things. For God is the beginning, that is the cause, of all creatures and the end because from him they receive and begin their being and to him they are moved so that they may find rest.

Love is the end and the quiet resting place for the natural restlessness of all things that are in motion, beyond which no further movement of the creature continues.

Deservedly, God is called love because He is the cause of all love, is spread through all things and gathers all things together into one and integrates them into Himself in an ineffable return, bringing to final completion in himself the loving motions of all creatures.

Going out into all things in order, God makes all things and is made all in all, and returns into Himself, calling back all things into Himself, and while He is made in all things, he does not cease to be above all things. And this is made manifest by the return of all things into the cause from which they proceeded, when all things will be converted back into God just as air is transmuted into light, when God will be all in all.

For God will be all in all and all creatures, absorbed as it were into God, will become overshadowed like stars as the sun rises.

15 THE VOYAGE OF ST BRENDAN: THE ISLAND OF THE BLESSED
c. 900–950 CE

The voyage of the sixth-century Irish monk Brendan of Clonfert across the western seas in search of the island of the blessed provides the subject matter for one of the most popular medieval legends. First recounted in a manuscript dating from the early tenth century, the story has been interpreted in several ways, including as an allegory of the monastic life, but it seems most likely that it is designed to illustrate the journey from this world to the next.

In both pre- and post-Christian Celtic tradition, people went west towards the setting sun to die and the islands far out in the western sea were seen as lands without sickness, old age or death, the dwelling places of the immortal dead. This theme is picked up in the story of Brendan and his companions setting out from Ireland across the Atlantic to find what is variously described as the island of the blessed, the island of the saints, the promised land and paradise.

The extract opposite comes at the beginning of the story when Brendan is visited by a monk called Barinthus who recounts his own experience of discovering this island. Enthralled by his description, Brendan decides to follow his example and casts off from Ireland's west coast. After many adventures, he finally ends up on the island of the blessed, which has all the characteristics described by Barinthus.

There is much in this description which echoes the depiction of heaven in Revelation and in later Christian literature – the precious stones, bountiful fruit and river which must be crossed to access the promised land. It anticipates that other great allegory of the journey from earth to heaven, Bunyan's *Pilgrim's Progress* (**29**). Like Barinthus, Brendan and his companions meet a 'young man of resplendent features, and very handsome aspect' who tells them

> This is the land you have sought after for so long a time. The days of your earthly pilgrimage must soon draw to a close, when you may rest in peace among your saintly brethren. After many years this land will be made manifest to those who come after you, when days of tribulation may come upon the people of Christ.

My dear son led me to the western shore where there was a small boat and he said: 'Father, enter this boat and we will sail on to the west, towards the island called the Land of Promise of the Saints, which God will grant to those who succeed us in the latter days.' When we entered the boat and set sail, clouds over-shadowed us on every side, so dense that we could scarcely see the prow or the stern of the boat. After the lapse of an hour or so, a great light shone around us, and land appeared, spacious and grassy, bearing all manner of fruits. When the boat touched the shore we landed, and walked round about the island for fifteen days, yet could not reach the limits thereof. No plant saw we there without its flower; no tree without its fruit; and all the stones were precious gems. On the fifteenth day we discovered a river flowing from the west towards the east. Being at a loss what to do, though we wished to cross over it, we awaited the direction of the Lord. While we considered the matter, there appeared suddenly before us a man, shining with a great light, who, calling us by our names, addressed us thus: 'Welcome, worthy brothers, for the Lord has revealed to you the land He will grant unto His saints. There is one-half of the island up to this river, which you are not permitted to pass over; return, therefore, whence you came.'

When he had ceased to speak, we asked him his name, and whence he had come. But he said: 'Why do you ask these questions? Should you not rather inquire about this island. Such as you see it now, so has it continued from the beginning of the world. You have been here a year already without having anything to eat or drink, or being weighed down by sleep, or shrouded in the darkness of the night. Know then for certain that here it is for ever day, without a shadow of darkness, for the Lord Jesus Christ is the light thereof, and if men had not transgressed the commandment of God, in this land of delights would they have always dwelt.'

16 ST FRANCIS ON SISTER DEATH
c. 1225

St Francis's well-known 'Canticle of the Creatures' has been much taken up in recent years to underline the ecological and environmental dimension of Christianity. Pope Francis used it as the basis for his 2015 encyclical *Laudato Si'* on caring for creation.

It finds a place in this anthology because of its final verse, which puts death alongside the rushing wind, flowing water and mother earth as an aspect of creation to be welcomed and through which God can be praised. Francis (1182–1226) added this verse to his canticle when, wracked with pain and almost completely blind, he had a vision indicating that his sufferings on earth would soon be over. He died shortly afterwards at the age of 44.

The original text of this verse, in the Umbrian dialect which Francis spoke, is as follows.

> *Laudato si mi Signore, per sora nostra Morte corporale,*
> *da la quale nullu homo vivente pò skappare.*
> *Guai a quelli ke morrano ne le peccata mortali;*
> *beati quelli ke trouarà ne le Tue sanctissime uoluntati,*
> *ka la morte secunda no 'l farrà male.*

The familiar translation opposite by William Henry Draper (1855–1933) only covers the first two lines. Here is a more literal translation of the whole verse.

> *Praised be You, my Lord, through our Sister Bodily Death,*
> *from whom no living man can escape.*
> *Woe to him who dies in mortal sin;*
> *blessed are those who find your most holy will,*
> *for the second death will not do them harm.*

This is the first of several hymns and gospel songs in this anthology. Recent research published in *The Gerontologist* shows that listening to them makes older people less anxious about dying, regardless of their faith or lack of it. We should be singing more about death!

All creatures of our God and King,
lift up your voice and with us sing,
Alleluia, alleluia!
Thou burning sun with golden beam,
thou silver moon with softer gleam:
O praise him, O praise him,
Alleluia, alleluia, allelluia!

Thou rushing wind that art so strong,
ye clouds that sail in heaven along,
O praise him, alleluia!
Thou rising morn, in praise rejoice;
ye lights of evening, find a voice: (Refrain)

Thou flowing water, pure and clear,
make music for thy Lord to hear,
Alleluia, alleluia!
Thou fire, so masterful and bright,
that givest us both warmth and light: (Refrain)

Dear mother earth, who day by day
unfoldest blessings on our way,
O praise him, alleluia!
The flowers and fruits that in thee grow,
let them his glory also show: (Refrain)

And thou, most kind and gentle death,
waiting to hush our latest breath,
O praise him, alleluia!
Thou leadest home the child of God,
and Christ our Lord the way has trod: (Refrain)

17 RUMI ON DEATH AS THE STOREHOUSE OF ALL FORTUNES AND RICHES
c. 1250

Jalal al-Din Rumi (1207–1273) was a Persian Sunni Muslim and Sufi mystic. His poems have become extremely popular in the West and he is the best-selling poet in the United States. He wrote extensively and positively about death, to which he looked forward as a release of the immortal soul from the body and the prison of the self.

The original Persian version of the poem on the top of the opposite page is inscribed on the elaborately carved walnut wood sarcophagus in the green-domed mausoleum built to house Rumi's body in Konya in what is now Turkey. Its arresting imagery presents the grave as a curtain 'hiding the communion of Paradise' and death as a meeting rather than a parting. The setting of the sun and moon are not calamities but rather necessary preludes to their rising again.

Rumi here expounds the Islamic doctrine of resurrection, similar to that held by Christians, and the idea that the seed must fall into the ground and die if it is to grow, found in St John's Gospel (**9**). He also references the story, found in both the Quran and the Hebrew Bible and memorably brought to life in the musical *Joseph and the Amazing Technicolor Dreamcoat* of Joseph being thrown by his jealous brothers into a well from which he is recovered by a passing caravan.

In the lower extract opposite, which is entitled 'The Grief of the Dead', Rumi suggests that the grief felt by the dead is not on account of their having died but rather comes from not making death, with all its possibilities and riches, their central focus in life, and having instead concentrated on the insubstantial phantoms and shadows of this fleeting life. Once again, there are strong biblical echoes here of what Jesus says about storing up treasures in heaven rather than on earth (Matthew 16:19–20).

The image of the dead as being like foam flakes carried on the sea and cast on the shore, rather as dust is carried on the wind, recurs in another of Rumi's poems, which begins 'Love is a boundless ocean, in which the heavens are but a flake of foam'.

When my bier moveth on the day of death,
Think not my heart is in this world.
Do not weep for me and cry 'Woe, woe!'
Thou wilt fall in the devil's snare: that is woe.
When thou seest my hearse, cry not 'Parted, parted!',
Union and meeting are mine in that hour.
If thou commit me to the grave, say not 'Farewell, farewell!'
For the grave is a curtain hiding the communion of Paradise.
After beholding descent, consider resurrection;
Why should setting be injurious to the sun and moon?
To thee it seems a setting, but 'tis a rising;
Though the vault seems a prison, 'tis the release of the soul.
What seed went down into the earth but it grew?
Why this doubt of thine as regards the seed of man?
What bucket was lowered but it came out brimful?
Why should the Joseph of the spirit complain of the well?
Shut thy mouth on this side and open it beyond,
For in placeless air will be thy triumphal song.

The Prince of mankind (Muhammed) said truly that no one who has passed away from this world feels sorrow and regret for having died, nay, but he feels a hundred regrets for having missed the opportunity, saying to himself, 'Why did I not make death my object – death which is the store-house of all fortunes and riches, and why, through seeing double, did I fasten my lifelong gaze upon those phantoms that vanished at the fated hour?'

The grief of the dead is not on account of death; it is because they dwelt on the phenomenal forms of existence and never perceived that all this foam is moved and fed by the Sea. When the Sea has cast the foam-flakes on the shore, go to the graveyard and behold them! Say to them, 'Where is your swirling onrush now?' and hear them answer mutely, 'Ask this question of the Sea, not of us'. How should the foam fly without the wave? How should the dust rise to the zenith without the wind? Since you have seen the dust, see the Wind; since you have seen the foam, see the Ocean of Creative Energy.

18 RUMI, 'FONS VITAE'
c. 1250

This poem, in a free translation by the distinguished early twentieth-century scholar of Islamic mysticism Reynold Nicholson, employs the image of drops of water passing into the sea to describe death and what lies beyond it. It also expresses Rumi's conception of all creation as a great upward spiral of metamorphoses. Essentially, he is here expounding the theory of evolution with the emergence of successively higher levels of life, from minerals to humans via plants and animals. This circle of life, involving a series of deaths, is powered and undergirded by divine love. It is spelled out more fully in another of his poems:

> *I died as mineral and became a plant,*
> *I died as plant and rose to animal,*
> *I died as animal and I was man.*
> *Why should I fear? When was I less by dying?*
> *Yet once more I shall die as man, to soar*
> *With angels blest, but even from angelhood*
> *I must pass on. All except God doth perish.*
> *When I have sacrificed my angel-soul,*
> *I shall become what no mind e'er conceived.*
> *Oh, let me not exist! for non-existence*
> *Proclaims in organ tones 'To him we shall return'.*

Ultimately, the departed human soul passes beyond angelhood to a kind of non-existence. By this term Rumi means self-abandonment. The individual soul must utterly abandon its ego and die to self before it can shine within the divine life. He expresses this with the simple injunction 'die before you die'. In his poem 'The Life Everlasting' he uses similar language to Eriugena (14), likening reabsorption into the divine to stars being overshadowed in the presence of the sun:

> *Those who have passed from the world are not non-existent: they are*
> *steeped in the Divine Attributes.*
> *All their attributes are absorbed in the Attributes of God, even*
> *as stars vanish in the presence of the sun.*

Whilst far away the living fountains ply,
  Each petty brook goes brimful to the main,
Since brook nor fountain can for ever die,
Thy fears how foolish, thy lament how vain!

What is this fountain, wouldst thou rightly know?
The Soul whence issue all created things,
Doubtless the rivers shall not cease to flow
Till silenced are the everlasting springs.

Farewell to sorrow, and with quiet mind
Drink long and deep: let others fondly deem
The channel empty they perchance may find,
Or fathom that unfathomable stream.

The moment thou to this low world wast given,
A ladder stood whereby thou mightst aspire;
And first thy steps, which upward still have striven,
From the mineral mounted to the plant; then higher

To animal existence; next, the Man
With knowledge, reason, faith. O wondrous goal!
This body, which a crumb of dust began –
How fairly fashioned the consummate whole!

Yet stay not here thy journey: thou shalt grow
An angel bright and have thine home in Heaven.
Plod on, plunge last in the great Sea, that so
That little drop makes oceans seven times seven.

19 HOPES OF MEETING LOVED ONES IN HEAVEN

1535–1663

There is a long-held Christian belief that family and friends will be reunited in heaven. In their book *Heaven: A History*, Bernhard Lang and Colleen McDannell identify the earliest expression of this idea in the writings of Bishop Cyprian of Carthage in the mid-third century. [18]

In the first of the three strong assertions of this belief by devout Christians in the sixteenth and seventeenth centuries printed opposite, the Catholic statesman Thomas More adduces biblical evidence to support it. He cites the fact that Adam, despite having been cast by God into a 'dead sleep', knows Eve when she is created from his rib (Genesis 2:21–24), the story of the rich man lying in hell seeing Abraham and Lazarus afar off in heaven (Luke 16:23) and the appearance of Moses and Elijah to Peter, James and John at the transfiguration (Matthew 7:3).

Biblical characters also feature prominently in Katherine Stubbes' moving deathbed utterance expressing her certainty that 'we will know one another in the life to come'. The former Anglican turned Independent clergyman Richard Baxter (**25**) was moved to write about his belief in this doctrine at a time when he was, in his own words, 'silenced and cast out' and felt particularly lonely. The verses quoted opposite are found in his hymn 'He wants not friends that hath Thy love.'

The belief that friends and family would be reunited in heaven continued to be widespread in the eighteenth and nineteenth centuries. The evangelical politician and reformer William Wilberforce wrote in 1797:

> I have no doubt at all that they who, having known each other on earth, shall be made joint partakers of heavenly glory, will know each other in that blessed state. The foundation of this opinion is laid rather in the nature of things and in general reasoning than in particular passages of Scripture.

A hymn by James Montgomery contains the line 'There is a world above where parting is unknown' and Christina Rossetti writes of heaven 'There we shall meet as once we met and love with old familiar love'.

[18]   *Heaven: A History* (New Haven, Connecticut: Yale University Press, 1988), p. 61.

Farewell, my dear child, and pray for me, and I shall for you, and for all your friends, that we may merrily meet in heaven.

Thomas More writing to his daughter shortly before his execution for treason on 6 July 1535

I do most constantly believe, that my soul, so soon as ever it shall depart forth of my body, shall be carried by the ministry of the holy Angels of God, into the kingdom of Heaven where I shall see, and certainly know, Adam, Noah, Abraham, Isaac, Jacob, Moses, Samuel, David, and all other Prophets, Patriarchs and Fathers, together, with Mary the mother of Christ, Peter, Paul, James and John, and all other Martyrs, Confessors, and holy Saints of God.

What a comfortable thing is this, that we shall know one another in the life to come, talk one with another, love one another, and praise God one with another, and all together.

The last words of Katherine Stubbes, who died in childbirth at the age of 19 in 1590 (as recorded by her husband)

As for my friends, they are not lost:
The several vessels of thy fleet
Though parted now, by tempests tossed,
Shall safely in the haven meet.
We still are centred all in thee,
Though distant, members of one Head;
Within one family we be,
And by one faith and spirit led.
Before thy throne we daily meet
As joint-petitioners to thee;
In spirit each the other greet,
And shall again each other see.
The heavenly hosts, world without end,
Shall be my company above;
And thou, my best and surest Friend,
Who shall divide me from thy love?

Extract from a poem by Richard Baxter,
written in December 1663

20 JOHN DONNE ON THE PROGRESS OF THE SOUL
1612

The metaphysical poet and divine John Donne (1572–1631) was brought up in the Roman Catholic faith by his widowed mother. After many years of poverty and insecurity, he took Anglican orders in 1615 and spent the last ten years of his life as Dean of St Paul's Cathedral. He explored the theme of death and what lies beyond it in several of his sermons and poems, perhaps attracted to it because of recurrent bouts of severe illness.

'The Progress of the Soul', from which the extracts opposite are taken, was the second of two poems that Donne wrote celebrating Elizabeth Drury, the daughter of his patron Sir Robert Drury, following her death on the eve of her fifteenth birthday. It wonderfully evokes heaven approaching the dying person like a taper which gradually lights up a darkened room.

Donne skilfully turns the tell-tale signs of death into harbingers of hope and liberation. The labouring breaths become harmonious notes. The discomfort of lying 'loose and slack' on the deathbed is 'the unbinding of a pack' which will release the soul. The sounding of the death knell is the welcoming call of the church triumphant. He dramatically likens the soul leaving the body to a chick hatching from a broken eggshell or a bullet speeding from an old rusty gun. There are echoes of both Plato (**4**) and Cicero (**7**) in his emphasis on the liberty and enfranchisement that death brings.

Perhaps particularly powerful is the description here of death and the swift passage of the soul from earth to heaven as a third birth, following naturally after the first birth of creation/conception and the second birth of grace/baptism. It brings heaven as near and present to the dying Elizabeth Drury as the colours and objects in the room, which was previously all dark but is now lit with tapers.

Donne takes another tilt at death in a later sonnet which begins 'Death, be not proud, though some have called thee mighty and dreadful, for thou art not so' and ends 'One short sleep past, we wake eternally and death shall be no more; Death, thou shalt die.'

58

Think then, my soul, that death is but a groom,
   Which brings a taper to the outward room,
Whence thou spiest first a little glimmering light,
And after brings it nearer to thy sight;
For such approaches doth heaven make in death.
Think thyself labouring now with broken breath,
And think those broken and soft notes to be
Division, and thy happiest harmony.
Think thee laid on thy death-bed, loose and slack,
And think that but unbinding of a pack,
To take one precious thing, thy soul, from thence.
Think thyself parch'd with fever's violence;
Anger thine ague more, by calling it
Thy physic; chide the slackness of the fit.
Think that thou hear'st thy knell, and think no more,
But that, as bells call'd thee to church before,
So this to the Triumphant Church calls thee …
Think that death hath now enfranchised thee;
Thou hast thy expansion now, and liberty
Think that a rusty piece, discharged, is flown
In pieces, and the bullet is his own,
And freely flies; this to thy soul allow.
Think thy shell broke, think thy soul hatch'd but now.
And think this slow-paced soul which late did cleave
To a body, and went but by the body's leave,
Dispatches in a minute all the way
'Twixt heaven and earth …
As doth the pith, which, lest our bodies slack,
Strings fast the little bones of neck and back,
So by the soul doth death string heaven and earth;
For when our soul enjoys this her third birth
– Creation gave her one, a second grace –
Heaven is as near and present to her face
As colours are and objects in a room,
Where darkness was before, when tapers come.

21 THOMAS CAMPION, 'NEVER WEATHER-BEATEN SAIL MORE WILLING BENT TO SHORE' 1613

This is one of more than a hundred short songs with lute accompaniments written by Thomas Campion (1567–1620), who practised as a doctor in London until his death at the age of 53, possibly of the plague. It was set by C. H. Parry as one of his 'Songs of Farewell'.

Presenting striking images of the spirit flying out of the breast, the distinctive quality of light found in heaven, and the absence of 'cold age' there to deafen our ears or dim our eyes, it also beautifully invokes the much-used metaphor of sailing in a boat either, as here, towards the shore, or out into the ocean, but always into the loving embrace of God.

This image was employed in the account of the death in 1999 of the English Roman Catholic leader Cardinal Basil Hume by his private secretary, James Curry. Noticing a decline in Hume's condition, Curry anointed him and began the prayer of commendation which opens this anthology. 'As we prayed, he died. He was a man ready to die; impatient to see God. It was as if he lay in a boat and we gently gave that boat a nudge and it sailed into the presence of God.'

It is also used in an oft-quoted reflection on dying by Charles Brent (1862–1929), a bishop in the American Episcopal Church:

> I am standing on the seashore. A ship sails and spreads her white sails to the morning breeze and starts for the ocean. She is an object of beauty and I stand watching her till at last she fades on the horizon, and someone at my side says: 'She is gone.' Gone where? Gone from my sight, that is all; she is just as large in the masts, hull and spars as she was when I saw her, and just as able to bear her load of living freight to its destination.
>
> The diminished size and total loss of sight is in me, not her; and just at the moment when someone at my side says, 'She's gone,' there are others who are watching her coming and other voices take up a glad shout, 'There she comes' – and that is dying.

Never weather-beaten sail more willing bent to shore,
Never tired pilgrim's limbs affected slumber more,
Than my wearied sprite now longs to fly out of my troubled breast:
O come quickly, sweetest Lord, and take my soul to rest.

Ever blooming are the joys of Heaven's high Paradise.
Cold age deafs not there our ears nor vapour dims our eyes:
Glory there the sun outshines whose beams the blessed only see:
O come quickly, glorious Lord, and raise my sprite to thee!

22 JERUSALEM, MY HAPPY HOME
c. 1616

This picturesque depiction of the heavenly New Jerusalem, derived from the Book of Revelation (**10**), appears to date from the early seventeenth century. It is printed in an anonymous ballad text from that time in the British Library and the version quoted opposite comes from a Catholic Commonplace Book dated 1616. Alongside the familiar image of heaven as a 'happy harbour', the river and trees of life and the ever-singing angels, it portrays gates of orient pearl, 'exceeding rich and rare', streets paved with gold and houses made of ivory.

Here is a popular view of heaven, conceived in more gorgeous and graphic terms than in the abstract speculations of philosophers and theologians, which makes up in vivid imagery what it lacks in poetic sophistication, as exemplified in three of its other many verses:

> *Thy gardens and thy gallant walks*
> *Continually are green;*
> *There grow such sweet and pleasant flowers*
> *As nowhere else are seen.*

> *There lust and lucre cannot dwell*
> *There envy bears no sway;*
> *There is no hunger, heat, nor cold,*
> *But pleasure every way.*

> *Within thy gates no thing doth come*
> *That is not passing clean,*
> *No spider's web, nor dirt, not dust,*
> *No filth may there be seen.*

'Jerusalem, my happy home' has found its way into over eight hundred hymn books, some of which erroneously ascribe its authorship to St Augustine. The *English Hymnal* version has twenty-six verses. Other hymns give a similar view of heaven, notably two translations by John Mason Neale of medieval poems 'Jerusalem the Golden, with Milk and Honey Blest' and 'Blessed City, Heavenly Salem'.

Jerusalem, my happy home,
  When shall I come to thee?
When shall my sorrows have an end,
Thy joys when shall I see?

O happy harbour of the Saints!
O sweet and pleasant soil!
In thee no sorrow may be found,
No grief, no care, no toil.

In thee no sickness may be seen,
No hurt, no ache, no sore;
In thee there is no dread of death,
But life for evermore.

No dampish mist is seen in thee,
Nor cold nor darksome night;
There every soul shines as the sun,
There God himself gives light.

Quite through the streets, with silver sound,
The flood of Life doth flow;
Upon whose banks on every side
The wood of Life doth grow.

There trees for evermore bear fruit,
And evermore do spring;
There evermore the angels sit,
And evermore do sing.

Jerusalem, my happy home,
Would God I were in thee!
Would God my woes were at an end,
Thy joys that I might see!

23 JOHN DONNE, TWO SERMONS ON DEATH
1627

These two extracts from sermons preached by John Donne towards the end of his life reiterate the positive and hopeful view of death expressed in 'The Progress of the Soul' (**20**).

The first, from a sermon delivered at Whitehall on the first Sunday of Lent, contains the powerful description of entering the gate of heaven to find 'one equal light' and 'one equal music', which has rightly become a favourite reading and prayer in funeral services and which I have myself read to those anxious about approaching death. It is also notable for its reference to the biblical story of Jacob's dream (Genesis 28:10–22) and its very clear depiction of death as a state of sleep from which God will eventually awaken us. Here Donne follows Martin Luther, who wrote

> It is probable, in my opinion, that, with very few exceptions indeed, the dead sleep in utter insensibility till the day of judgement. On what authority can it be said that the souls of the dead may not sleep in the same way that the living pass in profound slumber the interval between their downlying at night and their uprising in the morning? [19]

The second extract comes from a sermon preached on Easter Sunday in St Paul's Cathedral. Its opening observation anticipates the oft-quoted statement by the Anglican divine Henry Scott Holland in a sermon delivered in 1910 when the body of King Edward VII was lying in state in Westminster Hall: 'Death is nothing at all. I have only slipped away into the next room.' It ends with a ringing affirmation of the closeness of the church militant on earth and the church triumphant in heaven and the conviction that we shall all sing together in one choir.

Donne rose from his sickbed to deliver his final sermon, 'Death's Duel', at St Paul's in February 1631 just six weeks before he died. An extended meditation on death, portrayed as the condition of humans when in their mothers' wombs, an ever-present part of life, and a liberating dying and rising with Christ, it ends 'Lie down in peace in his grave, till he vouchsafe you a resurrection, and an ascension into that kingdom which he hath prepared for you.'

19 Letter to Nicholas Amsdorf, Jan. 13, 1522, quoted in Jules Michelet, *The Life of Luther,* trans. William Hazlitt (London: W.G.Bohn,1862) p. 133

So then, the death of the righteous is a sleep. Those that sleep in Jesus Christ will God bring with him; not only fetch them out of the dust when he comes, but bring them with him, that is, declare that they have been in his hands ever since they departed out of this world. They shall awake as Jacob did, and say as Jacob said, Surely the Lord is in this place, and this is no other but the house of God, and the gate of heaven, and into that gate they shall enter, and in that house they shall dwell, where there shall be no cloud nor sun, no darkness nor dazzling, but one equal light, no noise nor silence, but one equal music, no fears nor hopes, but one equal possession, no foes nor friends, but an equal communion and identity, no ends nor beginnings, but one equal eternity. Keep us Lord so awake in the duties of our callings, that we may thus sleep in thy peace, and wake in thy glory, and change that infallibility which thou affordest us here, to an actual and undeterminable possession of that kingdom which thy Son our Saviour Christ Jesus hath purchased for us, with the inestimable price of his incorruptible blood. Amen.

We think not a friend lost, because he has gone into another room, nor because he has gone into another land: and into another world, no man has gone; for that Heaven, which God created, and this world, is all one world. If I had fixed a son in Court, or married a daughter into a plentiful fortune, I were satisfied for that son and that daughter. Shall I not be so, when the King of Heaven hath taken that son to himself, and married himself to that daughter, for ever? I spend none of my faith, I exercise none of my hope, in this, that I shall have my dead raised to life again.

This is the faith that sustains me, when I lose by the death of others, or when I suffer by living in misery myself: that the dead and we are now all in one Church, and at the resurrection, shall be all in one choir.

24 GEORGE HERBERT ON DEATH
1633

George Herbert (1593–1633) was a gentle Anglican country clergyman who enjoyed only three years as rector of Bemerton in Wiltshire before his untimely death at the age of 40. He is remembered today for such hymns as 'Teach me my God and king' and 'King of glory, king of peace'.

His poem about death begins with a stark evocation of its grim reality in terms of flesh being turned into dust and bones to sticks. It is reminiscent of those graphic carvings of skulls and skeletons serving as a *memento mori* found on gravestones in churchyards.

But this is a depiction of death as it was before Jesus' death and resurrection, which have changed everything. No longer 'an uncouth hideous thing', death has grown 'fair and full of grace' and even become 'much in request' and 'much sought for as a good'.

This appreciation of the positive aspect of death is predicated on the fact that at 'Doomsday' souls will 'wear their new array' and bones 'with beauty shall be clad'. There are echoes here of the prophet Ezekiel's vision of the valley of dry bones which God miraculously clothes with flesh, covers with skin and breathes new life into (Ezekiel 37) and of Isaiah's promise of 'garlands instead of ashes' and 'garments of splendour for the heavy heart' (Isaiah 61:3). A more direct influence is St Paul's description of resurrection in 1 Corinthians (**8**).

So we no longer need fear death but can approach it as we do sleep, looking forward to lying in our graves with pillows of dust as we might lie in our beds with pillows of down, the soft underfeathers of ducks and geese which used to stuff pillows and mattresses.

A similar message is conveyed in a poem by Herbert's contemporary, Sir Thomas Browne:

> *Sleep is a death; O make me try,*
> *By sleeping, what it is to die!*
> *And as gently lay my head*
> *On my grave as now my bed.*

Death, thou wast once an uncouth hideous thing,
  Nothing but bones,
The sad effect of sadder groans:
Thy mouth was open, but thou couldst not sing.

For we considered thee as at some six
Or ten years hence,
After the loss of life and sense,
Flesh being turned to dust, and bones to sticks.

We looked on this side of thee, shooting short;
Where we did find
The shells of fledge souls left behind,
Dry dust, which sheds no tears, but may extort.

But since our Saviour's death did put some blood
Into thy face,
Thou art grown fair and full of grace,
Much in request, much sought for as a good.

For we do now behold thee gay and glad,
As at Doomsday;
When souls shall wear their new array,
And all thy bones with beauty shall be clad.

Therefore we can go die as sleep, and trust
Half that we have
Unto an honest faithful grave;
Making our pillows either down, or dust.

25 Richard Baxter, 'The Saints' Everlasting Rest' 1649

This extended meditation on heaven, written during a period of severe illness and depression when the author felt himself near to death, became a devotional classic.

Richard Baxter (1615–1691) was ordained into the Church of England in 1638 but found himself increasingly out of sympathy with its episcopal form of government and in many respects closer to Nonconformist dissenters. He served as a minister in Kidderminster, Worcestershire, from 1641 to 1660, with spells away acting as a chaplain to the soldiers in Oliver Cromwell's army during the English Civil War. After the restoration of the monarchy in 1660 he was offered the bishopric of Hereford but turned it down and took to preaching in London in independent meeting houses, which were declared illegal conventicles under the terms of the Act of Uniformity. He suffered considerable persecution and was imprisoned for eighteen months in 1685.

Baxter's stormy life is reflected in the way that he envisages heaven as an eirenic haven where 'we shall rest from all our sad divisions and unchristian quarrels with one another'. Although he pictures heaven primarily in terms of rest from labour and relief from quarrelling, suffering and sickness, he emphasizes that it is not a static state but rather one of 'sweet and constant action of all the powers of the soul and body in the enjoyment of God'. He singles out singing as one of the main activities in which the saints will engage there.

Above all, Baxter's vision of heaven is theocentric, focused on the worship, enjoyment and presence of God. He makes clear that only those who are regenerate and righteous will enjoy the saints' rest found there. Unregenerate sinners will 'lose the enjoyments of time and suffer the torments of Hell', torments which he insists will be eternal and without mitigation. While the reality of judgement and a clear distinction between the saved and the damned loom large in his conception of the afterlife, the overall message of *The Saints' Everlasting Rest* is that Christians should meditate earnestly and continually on heaven throughout their lives and prepare themselves for it, not least through hearty singing in church.

Look not on the dead bones, and dust, and difficulty, but at the promise. Contentedly commit these carcasses to a prison that shall not long contain them. Let us lie down in peace and take our rest; it will not be an everlasting night, nor endless sleep.

This rest contains a sweet and constant action of all the powers of the soul and body in the enjoyment of God. It is not the rest of the stone, which ceaseth from all motion when it attains the centre. The memory will not be idle, or useless. We will rejoice in our God with joy, and rest in our love and joy in Him with singing.

We shall live in our own element. We are now as the fish in a vessel of water, only so much as will keep them alive; but what is that to the ocean? We have a little air let into us, to afford us breathing; but what is that to the sweet and fresh gales upon Mount Sion? We have a beam of the sun to lighten up darkness, and a warm ray to keep us from freezing; but then we shall live in its light, and be revived by its heat for ever.

We shall rest from all our sad divisions and unchristian quarrels with one another. How lovingly do thousands live together in heaven, who lived at variance upon earth! There is no contention, because none of this pride, ignorance, or other corruption.

We shall rest from all our now personal sufferings. This may seem a small thing to those who live in ease and prosperity; but to the daily afflicted soul it makes the thought of heaven delightful. Oh the dying life we now live, as full of sufferings as of days and hours! Oh the blessed tranquillity of that region, where there is nothing but sweet continued peace! O healthful place, where none are sick! O happy land, where all are kings! O holy assembly, where all are priests! Our faces shall no more be pale or sad, no more breaches in friendship, nor parting of friends asunder; no more trouble accompanying our relations, nor voice of lamentation heard in our dwellings. We shall rest from all the toil of duties.

26 HENRY VAUGHAN, 'THE WATERFALL' 1655

This poem by the Welsh metaphysical poet and medical practitioner Henry Vaughan (1621–1695) evokes the journey from life to death by employing the familiar imagery of a river passing into the sea. In this case, it is a waterfall which provides a metaphor for the soul's passage into eternity with the water moving with increasing momentum toward the brink and briefly hesitating before taking the plunge over the precipice 'where, clear as glass, all must descend' not to an end, but to a longer, smoother and more gentle course. Watching the waterfall and reflecting how every drop of water runs where it flowed before and ultimately returns to its source, the poet asks why 'frail flesh' should 'doubt any more that what God takes, he'll not restore'.

Death here is presented as something entirely natural which should not be feared or resisted. It is only to be expected that we are afraid of the 'steep place' and the 'deep and rocky grave' but, like the water, we pass over it to achieve a deeper and calmer flow in the 'sea of light' from which we came. No longer agitated, chiding and calling, but rather 'quickened' and made truly alive, we 'rise to a longer course more bright and brave'.

'The Waterfall' reflects a theme found in several of Henry Vaughan's poems and reminiscent of John Scotus Eriugena's idea of 'ineffable return' (14): death as a return to the source and the beginning. It is dramatically expressed at the end of his poem 'The Retreat' (1650):

> Some men a forward motion love,
> But I by backward steps would move,
> And when this dust falls to the urn
> In that state I came return.

With what deep murmurs through time's silent stealth
    Doth thy transparent, cool, and wat'ry wealth
Here flowing fall,
And chide, and call,
As if his liquid, loose retinue stay'd
Ling'ring, and were of this steep place afraid;
The common pass
Where, clear as glass,
All must descend
Not to an end,
But quicken'd by this deep and rocky grave,
Rise to a longer course more bright and brave.

Dear stream! dear bank, where often I
Have sat and pleas'd my pensive eye,
Why, since each drop of thy quick store
Runs thither whence it flow'd before,
Should poor souls fear a shade or night,
Who came, sure, from a sea of light?
Or since those drops are all sent back
So sure to thee, that none doth lack,
Why should frail flesh doubt any more
That what God takes, he'll not restore?

27 HENRY VAUGHAN, 'DEAR, BEAUTEOUS DEATH' 1655

The verses opposite form part of a longer poem which Henry Vaughan wrote when he was particularly conscious of the deaths of several of those close to him, including his younger brother, William, who had died in 1648, possibly as a result of wounds sustained while fighting in the English Civil War. It begins:

> *They are all gone into the world of light!*
> *And I alone sit ling'ring here;*
> *Their very memory is fair and bright,*
> *And my sad thoughts doth clear.*

> *I see them walking in an air of glory,*
> *Whose light doth trample on my days:*
> *My days, which are at best but dull and hoary,*
> *Mere glimmering and decays.*

Both this poem and 'The Waterfall' (**26**) were written in the aftermath of a prolonged and painful illness, which made Henry Vaughan acutely conscious of his own mortality and resolved him to turn away from what he came to see as a misspent youth. He underwent a dramatic religious conversion and, strongly influenced by his friend George Herbert, turned from secular to sacred verse, adopting the motto *moriendo, revixi* (by dying, I gain new life).

There are distinct echoes in 'Dear, beauteous Death!' of Herbert's poem 'Death' (**24**). Both poets use similar language to encourage us to look beyond the dust and bones, with Herbert counselling against 'shooting short' and Vaughan expressing the hope that we 'outlook that mark'. They also both use the imagery of fledging birds hatching from their eggs and fleeing their nests to describe death and the mystery of what lies beyond it.

Vaughan's approach is more mystical and ecstatic. Invoking angels and stars, he describes death as 'the jewel of the just' shining in the dark.

Dear, beauteous Death! the jewel of the just,
Shining nowhere, but in the dark;
What mysteries do lie beyond thy dust
Could man outlook that mark!

He that hath found some fledg'd bird's nest, may know
At first sight, if the bird be flown;
But what fair well or grove he sings in now,
That is to him unknown.

And yet as angels in some brighter dreams
Call to the soul, when man doth sleep:
So some strange thoughts transcend our wonted themes
And into glory peep.

If a star were confin'd into a tomb,
Her captive flames must needs burn there;
But when the hand that lock'd her up, gives room,
She'll shine through all the sphere.

O Father of eternal life, and all
Created glories under thee!
Resume thy spirit from this world of thrall
Into true liberty.

Either disperse these mists, which blot and fill
My perspective still as they pass,
Or else remove me hence unto that hill,
Where I shall need no glass.

28 ABRAHAM COWLEY, 'A DESCRIPTION OF HEAVEN'
1656

These verses come from a long poem about David and Saul by the leading seventeenth-century English poet and staunch royalist Abraham Cowley (1618–1667).

In many ways his is a very literal and old-fashioned view of heaven as a physical place located high up above the sky where God Almighty sits on his throne, the incomprehensible creator, sustainer and ruler of all, surrounded by armies of angels endlessly singing his praise.

What is particularly striking and most appealing about Cowley's vision of heaven is its sense of order and harmony. He very much espouses the notion of the music of the spheres, which is found in much later seventeenth- and early eighteenth-century poetry and is perhaps most elegantly expressed in Joseph Addison's hymn 'The Spacious Firmament on High'. Similar language is found in one of the first poems that Henry Vaughan wrote following his religious conversion, 'The World' (1650), which begins with this mystical evocation of the life to come:

> I saw Eternity the other night,
> Like a great ring of pure and endless light,
> All calm, as it was bright,
> And round beneath it, Time in hours, days, years
> Driv'n by the spheres
> Like a vast shadow mov'd; in which the world
> And all her train were hurl'd.

Perhaps the most memorable image of heaven in Cowley's poem is contained in the lines:

> Nothing is there to come, and nothing past,
> But an eternal now does always last.

This beautifully conveys the idea of there being no time as we understand it in heaven, but rather a constant present or 'eternal now'. It is the state that techniques of mindfulness attempt to direct us towards in this life.

A bove the subtle foldings of the sky,
Above the well-set orbs' soft harmony,
Above those petty lamps that guild the night;
There is a place o'erflown with hallowed light;
Where Heaven, as if it left it self behind,
Is stretched out far, nor its own bounds can find:
Here peaceful flames swell up the sacred place,
Nor can the glory contain itself in th'endless space.
For there no twilight of the sun's dull ray
Glimmers upon the pure and native day.
No pale-faced moon does in stolen beams appear,
Or with dim taper scatters darkness there.
On no smooth sphere the restless seasons slide,
No circling motion doth swift tint divide;
Nothing is there to come, and nothing past,
But an eternal now does always last.
There sits the Almighty, First of all, and End;
Whom nothing but Himself can comprehend.
Who with his Word commanded all to be,
And all obeyed him, for that Word was He.
Only he spoke, and every thing that is
From out the womb of fertile Nothing ris.
Oh who shall tell, who shall describe thy throne,
Thou great Three One?
There Thou thy self do'st in full presence show,
Not absent from these meaner Worlds below ...

For his spirit contains
The well-knit Mass, from him each creature gains
Being and motion, which he still bestows;
From him the effect of our weak action flows.
Round him vast armies of swift angels stand,
Which seven triumphant generals command,
They sing loud anthems of his endless praise,
And with fixed eyes drink in immortal rays.

29 JOHN BUNYAN, *THE PILGRIM'S PROGRESS* 1678

This splendid evocation of the joys of heaven comes from one of the classic works of English literature and spiritual devotion. Its author, John Bunyan (1628–1688), underwent a religious conversion while practising his father's trade as a tinker, travelling round mending pots and pans. He heard a voice from on high asking him 'Wilt thou leave thy sins and go to Heaven or have thy sins and go to Hell?' He joined a Nonconformist congregation in his native Bedford and endured two periods of imprisonment, the first lasting twelve years, for preaching in a dissenting conventicle.

It was during his imprisonment that Bunyan wrote *The Pilgrim's Progress*, which describes the journey of the Christian soul through the dangers and temptations of this life to its eventual destination in heaven. It is presented in the form of an allegorical dream in which the central character, Christian, travels from the City of Destruction to the Celestial City. He is joined by fellow-pilgrim Hopeful and together, after many adventures and vicissitudes, they reach their heavenly home.

Perhaps the best-known passage in the book, quite often read at funeral services, is that describing Christian and Hopeful crossing the deep river which separates this world from the next. I have chosen the passage that follows shortly afterwards when two 'Shining Ones' appear to the two pilgrims and tell them all about the Heavenly City, which they are about to enter.

Bunyan's view of heaven is clearly based on the descriptions in the Book of Revelation (**10**). He emphasizes the tree of life with its never fading fruits, the white robes that all will wear, the closeness to God and the unceasing praise and worship that will surround Him. There is also a clear affirmation that friends and family will be reunited, a belief that Bunyan also expressed in a poem of 1665:

> *Our friends that lived godly here,*
> *Shall there be found again;*
> *The wife, the child, and father dear,*
> *With others of the train.*

You are going now to the paradise of God, wherein you shall see the tree of life, and eat of the never-fading fruits thereof; and when you come there, you shall have white robes given you, and your walk and talk shall be every day with the King, even all the days of eternity. There you shall not see again such things as you saw when you were in the lower region upon the earth, to wit, sorrow, sickness, affliction, and death, for the former things are passed away. You are now going to Abraham, to Isaac, and Jacob, and to the prophets – men that God hath taken away from the evil to come, and that are now resting upon their beds, each one walking in his righteousness.

The men then asked, What must we do in the holy place? To whom it was answered, You must there receive the comforts of all your toil, and have joy for all your sorrow; you must reap what you have sown, even the fruit of all your prayers, and tears, and sufferings for the King by the way. In that place you must wear crowns of gold, and enjoy the perpetual sight and vision of the Holy One, for there you shall see him as he is. There also you shall serve him continually with praise, with shouting, and thanksgiving, whom you desired to serve in the world, though with much difficulty, because of the infirmity of your flesh. There your eyes shall be delighted with seeing, and your ears with hearing the pleasant voice of the Mighty One. There you shall enjoy your friends again that are gone thither before you; and there you shall with joy receive, even every one that follows into the holy place after you. There also shall you be clothed with glory and majesty, and put into an equipage fit to ride out with the King of Glory. When he shall come with sound of trumpet in the clouds, as upon the wings of the wind, you shall come with him; and when he shall sit upon the throne of judgment; you shall sit by him.

30 WILLIAM PENN, DEATH IS BUT CROSSING THE WORLD 1682

William Penn (1644–1718) was one of the earliest and most active members of the Religious Society of Friends who broke away from the Church of England in the mid-seventeenth century over their espousal of the doctrine of the priesthood of all believers and became known as Quakers. He founded the North American colony of Pennsylvania, which began as a settlement of English Quakers.

Penn's musings on death are to be found in his book *Some Fruits of Solitude*, which was almost certainly written during one of the periods of imprisonment in the Tower of London that he suffered because of his dissenting faith. While acknowledging that death is 'a dark passage', his understanding of it is almost uniformly positive and deeply reassuring. Describing it as a 'turning of us over from time to eternity' and likening it to a crossing of the sea, he seems to have believed in a direct passage of good souls to eternal life – 'they live as soon as they die' – without any intervening period of sleep or any general resurrection.

Like many of his contemporaries, Penn also clearly believed in the reuniting of friends in heaven. He goes on to suggest that the many different denominational masks which we wear on earth will there be removed and that we will no longer be strangers because we have espoused different beliefs and faiths but come to realise that we are all of one religion. In this he echoes Richard Baxter's view that 'we shall rest from our sad divisions and unchristian quarrels with one another' (**25**).

Penn's acceptance of death as a natural condition and part of life and his insistence that we must embrace it if we are properly to live is reflected in the current edition of the guidance published for members of the Religious Society of Friends in Britain, *Advices and Queries*, which asks: 'Are you able to contemplate your death and the death of those closest to you?' and continues: 'Accepting the fact of death, we are freed to live more fully'.[20]

---

[20] *Advices and Queries* (Yearly Meeting of the Religious Society of Friends, 2015), p.30

Though death be a dark passage, it leads to immortality, and that's recompense enough for suffering of it. And yet faith lights us, even through the grave, being the evidence of things not seen. And this is the comfort of the good, that the grave cannot hold them, and that they live as soon as they die.

Death is no more than a turning of us over from time to eternity. Nor can there be a revolution without it; for it supposes the dissolution of one form, in order to the succession of another.

Death then, being the way and condition of life, we cannot love to live, if we cannot bear to die.

They that love beyond the world cannot be separated by it. Death cannot kill what never dies. Nor can spirits ever be divided that love and live in the same Divine Principle; the root and record of their friendship. If absence be not death, neither is theirs.

Death is but crossing the world, as friends do the seas; they live in one another still. For they must needs be present, that love and live in that which is omnipresent.

In this Divine Glass, they see face to face; and their converse is free, as well as pure.

This is the comfort of friends, that though they may be said to die, yet their friendship and society are, in the best sense, ever present, because immortal.

The humble, meek, merciful, just, pious, and devout souls are everywhere of one religion; and when death has taken off the mask they will know one another, though the divers liveries they wear here makes them strangers.

31

ISAAC WATTS, 'THERE IS A LAND OF PURE DELIGHT' 1709

Often called the father of English hymnody, Isaac Watts (1674–1748) ministered in an Independent church in London until his health broke down. His many hymns include Christian versions of the Psalms, such as 'O God, our help in ages past' and 'When I survey the wondrous Cross', the first known hymn in the English language to include the personal pronoun 'I' and to express the experience of Christian faith rather than limiting itself to matters of doctrine.

'There Is a Land of Pure Delight' presents an idyllic picture of heaven as a place where everlasting spring abides and infinite day excludes the night. Yet timorous mortals shrink from crossing the narrow sea that divides this heavenly land from ours and linger shivering on the bank, fearing to launch away. In this powerful image, Watts recalls Henry Vaughan's description of the water lingering before rushing over the precipice of the waterfall, being 'of this steep place afraid' (**26**).

The portrayal of death as a journey across a river or sea is found in many cultures. The Yoruba people of Nigeria bury their dead in canoes to prepare them for their journey across one or more rivers to enter the next world. In Greek mythology the ferryman Charon transported souls across the river Styx, which encircled the Underworld and formed the boundary between the worlds of the living and the dead. The Buddha is often portrayed in similar terms as a ferryman and one of his discourses compares monks crossing Mara's stream to make the journey from life to death to cattle crossing the river Ganga (Ganges) and arriving safe on the further shore. In 'The Pilgrim's Progress' Christian and Hopeful have to wade through a deep river to reach the Celestial City (**29**) and in 'Crossing the Bar' Tennyson uses the image of crossing the sandbar to catch the tide where the river meets the sea (**55**).

Many hymns present heaven in similar terms to Watts as a land of pure delight. A prime example is one for children by Andrew Young, which begins:

> There is a happy land, far, far away,
> Where Saints in glory stand, bright, bright as day.

There is a land of pure delight,
where saints immortal reign;
infinite day excludes the night,
and pleasures banish pain.

There everlasting spring abides,
and never-withering flowers;
death, like a narrow sea, divides
that heavenly land from ours.

Sweet fields beyond the swelling flood
stand dressed in living green;
so to the Jews old Canaan stood,
while Jordan rolled between.

But timorous mortals start and shrink
to cross the narrow sea,
and linger shivering on the brink,
and fear to launch away.

O could we make our doubts remove,
those gloomy doubts that rise,
and see the Canaan that we love
with unbeclouded eyes;

Could we but climb where Moses stood,
and view the landscape o'er,
not Jordan's stream, nor death's cold flood,
should fright us from the shore!

32 Dr Johnson on Our Situation in a Future State
1772

This extract from James Boswell's *Life of Samuel Johnson* records a conversation between the two men one evening in March 1772. It gives an interesting insight into Dr Johnson's view of 'a future state' and indicates that while well aware of the dangers of idle speculation, he felt it was reasonable to hope for a happy and fulfilling afterlife.

Dr Johnson had a life-long fear of death. He told Boswell that 'he never had a moment in which death was not terrible to him' and that 'the whole of life is but keeping away the thoughts of it'. Yet his Christian faith made him trust in the eternal love and mercy of God. He commented during his 1773 tour of the Hebrides:

> No wise man will be contented to die, if he thinks he is to go into a state of punishment. Nay, no wise man will be contented to die, if he thinks he is to fall into annihilation: for however unhappy any man's existence may be, he yet would rather have it, than not exist at all. No, there is no rational principle by which a man can die contented, but a trust in the mercy of God, through the merits of Jesus Christ.

In the conversation recorded opposite, Dr Johnson makes clear his view that the post-mortem existence is one of disembodied spirits rather than resurrected bodies, although not so spiritualized that there is no room for material pleasures such as music. His is an intellectual's vision of heaven where happiness will consist in 'a consciousness of the favour of God, the contemplation of truth and the possession of felicitating ideas'. In response to Boswell's suggestion that one of the most pleasant aspects of the afterlife will be seeing our friends again, Johnson gives a characteristically jaundiced and honest reply about just how flimsy or ill-advised many friendships are and suggests that only those that have real value will remain. He hedges his bets by reflecting that 'we shall either have the satisfaction of meeting our friends, or be satisfied without meeting them' and offers hope to those who may not be looking forward to reuniting with all their relations.

I visited him at night. Finding him in a very good humour, I ventured to lead him to the subject of our situation in a future state, having much curiosity to know his notions on that point.

JOHNSON: Why, Sir, the happiness of an unembodied spirit will consist in a consciousness of the favour of God, in the contemplation of truth, and in the possession of felicitating ideas.

BOSWELL: But, Sir, is there any harm in our forming to ourselves conjectures as to the particulars of our happiness, though the Scripture has said but very little on the subject? 'We know not what we shall be.'

JOHNSON: Sir, there is no harm. What philosophy suggests to us on this topic is probable: what scripture tells us is certain.

BOSWELL: One of the most pleasing thoughts is, that we shall see our friends again.

JOHNSON: Yes, Sir; but you must consider, that when we are become purely rational, many of our friendships will be cut off. Many friendships are formed by a community of sensual pleasures: all these will be cut off. We form many friendships with bad men, because they have agreeable qualities, and they can be useful to us; but, after death, they can no longer be of use to us. We form many friendships by mistake, imagining people to be different from what they really are. After death, we shall see everyone in a true light. Then, Sir, they talk of our meeting our relations: but then all relationship is dissolved; and we shall have no regard for one person more than another, but for their real value. However, we shall either have the satisfaction of meeting our friends, or be satisfied without meeting them.

BOSWELL: As to our employment in a future state, the sacred writings say little. The Revelation, however, of St. John gives us many ideas, and particularly mentions music.

JOHNSON: Why, Sir, ideas must be given you by means of something which you know: and as to music there are some philosophers and divines who have maintained that we shall not be spiritualized to such a degree, but that something of matter, very much refined, will remain. In that case, music may make a part of our future felicity.

33 WILLIAM WORDSWORTH, INTIMATIONS OF IMMORTALITY 1802–1804

William Wordsworth (1770–1850) is not the only writer to have suggested that, far from being like sleep, death is in fact a waking up from the real sleep which is our condition from birth and throughout life. The ancient Chinese philosopher Zhuang Zhou (c. 369–286 BCE) wrote in similar vein 'We are born from a quiet sleep and we die to a calm awakening' and Rumi argued that 'this world seems lasting, though 'tis but the sleeper's dream; who, when the appointed Day shall dawn, escapes from dark imaginings that haunted him, and turns with laughter on his phantom griefs when he beholds his everlasting home'.

For Wordsworth, 'heaven lies about us in our infancy' and 'our noisy years' of life on earth seem but 'moments in the being of the eternal Silence'. Echoing the philosophy of Eriugena (**14**), he states that we will eventually return to God, 'who is our home', and that in times of calm in this life we can glimpse 'that immortal sea which brought us hither' and see children sporting on its shore.

This is not the only time that Wordsworth has recourse to the familiar imagery of a sea of water to describe death and what lies beyond it. In his later poem 'The Excursion', published in 1814, he has an Anglican country parson reflect that the good and evil, the just and unjust all find 'a capacious bed and receptacle' and 'an equal resting place' in his churchyard.

> *Even as the multitude of kindred brooks*
> *And streams, whose murmur fills this hollow vale,*
> *Whether their course be turbulent or smooth,*
> *Their waters clear or sullied, all are lost*
> *Within the bosom of yon crystal Lake,*
> *And end their journey in the same repose!*

Here there is a sense of death bringing repose as much as awakening, as there is in his 1815 Epitaph quoted at the beginning of this book, which once again uses the imagery of the sea, in this case to describe life and our voyage to death as 'the quiet haven of us all'.

Our birth is but a sleep and a forgetting;
The Soul that rises with us, our life's Star,
Hath had elsewhere its setting
And cometh from afar;
Not in entire forgetfulness,
And not in utter nakedness,
But trailing clouds of glory do we come
From God, who is our home:
Heaven lies about us in our infancy!

Our noisy years seem moments in the being
Of the eternal Silence: truths that wake,
To perish never;
Which neither listlessness, nor mad endeavour,
Nor man nor boy,
Nor all that is at enmity with joy,
Can utterly abolish or destroy!
Hence, in a season of calm weather
Though inland far we be,
Our souls have sight of that immortal sea
Which brought us hither;
Can in a moment travel thither –
And see the children sport upon the shore,
And hear the mighty waters rolling evermore.

34 WILLIAM CHANNING ON THE FUTURE LIFE
1834

The American Unitarian minister William Channing (1780–1842) had no time for the traditional picture of heaven as a place of perpetual rest where white robed angels continually strum harps and sing praises around the throne of God. He looked forward to a much more bracing and active afterlife in which humanity continued to progress and develop. It was wrong, he wrote, to 'think of the future world as so happy that none need the aid of others, that effort ceases, that the good have nothing to do' and to 'imagine that the inhabitants of Heaven only rest and converse'. Rather, 'they who reach that world enter on a state of action, life and effort'.

As described here in an Easter Sunday sermon, preached following the death of a dear friend, Channing's heaven is a mixture of a university and hall of fame where the world's great and good are joined by those many unrecorded saints who have 'walked before God in the beauty of love and self-sacrificing virtue'. He was orthodox enough to believe that in heaven we will meet and converse with Christ but insisted that there will be nothing distant or subservient about our relationship with him there:

> Jesus is sometimes spoken of as reigning in the future world, and sometimes imagination places him on a real and elevated throne. Strange that such conceptions can enter the minds of Christians. Jesus will indeed reign in Heaven, and so he reigned on earth. He reigned in the fishing-boat, from which he taught; in the humble dwelling, where he gathered round him listening and confiding disciples. His reign is not the vulgar dominion of this world. Christ will not be raised on a throne above his followers. On earth he sat at the same table with the publican and sinner. Will he recede from the excellent whom he has fitted for celestial mansions?

Channing was also certain that those dwelling in heaven must retain their deepest interest in this world. Their ties to those they have left are not dissolved, but only refined. They go to Jesus Christ, the great lover of the human family.

We must not think of Heaven as a stationary community. I think of it as a world of stupendous plans and efforts for its own improvement. I think of it as a society passing through successive stages of development, virtue, knowledge, power, by the energy of its own members. There the work of education, which began here, goes on without end; and a diviner philosophy than is taught on earth, reveals the spirit to itself, and awakens it to earnest, joyful effort for its own perfection.

Heaven is, in truth, a glorious reality. Its attraction should be felt perpetually. It should over- come the force with which this world draws us to itself. Were there a country on earth uniting all that is beautiful in nature, all that is great in virtue, genius, and the liberal arts, and numbering among its citizens, the most illustrious patriots, poets, philosophers, philanthropists of our age, how eagerly should we cross the ocean to visit it! And how immeasurably greater is the attraction of Heaven. There live the elder brethren of the creation, the sons of the morning, who sang for joy at the creation of our race; there the great and good of all ages and climes; the friends, benefactors, deliverers, ornaments of their race; the patriarch, prophet, apostle, and martyr; the true heroes of public, and still more of private, life ; the father, mother, wife, husband, child, who, unrecorded by man, have walked before God in the beauty of love and self-sacrificing virtue. There are all who have built up in our hearts the power of goodness and truth, the writers from whose pages we have received the inspiration of pure and lofty sentiments, the friends whose countenances have shed light through our dwellings, and peace and strength through our hearts.

There they are gathered together, safe from every storm, triumphant over evil; and they say to us, Come and join us in our everlasting blessedness; Come and take part in our song of praise; Share our adoration, friendship, progress, and works of love. They say to us, Cherish now in your earthly life, that spirit and virtue of Christ which is the beginning and dawn of Heaven, and we shall soon welcome you, with more than human friendship, to our own immortality.

35 John Henry Newman, 'Waiting for the Morning' 1835

Although written just a year later, John Henry Newman's poem on heaven could not be more different from William Channing's sermon on the subject (**34**). In contrast to the American Unitarian's emphasis on strenuous activity and intellectual effort, the Anglican cleric paints a picture of rest, repose and meek musing.

When he wrote this poem, Newman (1801–1890) was vicar of the university church in Oxford and had recently embarked on his *Tracts for the Times*, setting in train the Tractarian movement to take the Church of England back to its Catholic roots. Newman's growing unease with Anglicanism was to lead eventually to his reception into the Roman Catholic church in 1845.

His portrayal of heaven, complete with mountain grots, haunted gardens, angelic forms and seraphic choirs, is romantic, archaic and reassuring. The main focus of his poem is on the four-fold river of paradise, mentioned in Genesis 2:10–14 in connection with the garden of Eden, which is described as sweeping down 'the dark and savage vale' and blending with neighbouring waters as they glide along. As for Henry Vaughan describing 'The Waterfall' (**26**), there is nothing to fear or provoke dismay in the flow of this giant stream. The effect of its sound and flow is rather to soothe and reassure.

The title 'Waiting for the Morning' perhaps hints at expectation of the Beatific Vision, the direct perception of God enjoyed by those in heaven, which is especially emphasized in Catholic doctrine. It is this vision that the souls in paradise are awaiting. The closing couplet of Newman's poem 'Lead, kindly light', written two years earlier, which describes the arrival of morning after a long dark night, could possibly be taken as another reference to the heavenly state and what awaits us there:

And with the morn those angel faces smile,
Which I have loved long since, and lost a while.

They are at rest:
    We may not stir the heaven of their repose
With loud-voiced grief or passionate request,
    Or selfish plaint for those
Who in the mountain grots in Eden lie,
And hear the four-fold river, as it hurries by.

They hear it sweep
    In distance down the dark and savage vale;
But they at eddying pool or current deep
    Shall never more grow pale;
They hear, and meekly muse, as fain to know
How long untired, unspent, that giant stream shall flow.

And soothing sounds
    Blend with the neighbouring waters as they glide;
Posted along the haunted garden's bounds
    Angelic forms abide,
Echoing, as words of watch, o'er lawn and grove,
The verses of that hymn which Seraphs chant above.

36 Christina Rossetti, 'Dream Land' 1849

The Victorian poet Christina Rossetti (1830–1892) was preoccupied with death from adolescence, probably partly because she suffered ill health from the age of 15. A devout Anglo-Catholic, she was described by fellow-poet Edmund Gosse as 'a cloistered spirit, timid, nun-like, bowed down by suffering and humility'.

She wrote several poems like this one, penned when she was 19, describing a female in a state which appears somewhere between deep sleep and death. What seems to start as a 'charmed sleep' becomes deeper and deeper and not to be woken from. The references to her face being 'toward the west' and to 'sleep that no pain shall wake' suggest that the subject of the poem is indeed experiencing the sleep-like rest from the toils and travails of life that comes with death.

Coloured illustrations that Christina Rossetti made to accompany this poem show a somewhat sepulchral-looking figure, clad in white and holding a cross, leaving behind the steep slope of a purple hill and ascending in winged form. A sonnet written at the same time as 'Dream Land' and entitled 'Life Hidden' makes an even more explicit connection between sleep and death:

> Roses and lilies grow above the place
> Where she sleeps the long sleep that doth not dream.
> If we could look upon her hidden face
> Nor shadow would be there nor garish gleam
> Of light: her life is lapsing like a stream
> That makes no noise but floweth on apace
> Seawards; while many a shade and shady beam
> Vary the ripples in their gliding chase.
> She doth not see, but knows: she doth not feel,
> And yet is sensible: she hears no sound,
> Yet counts the flight of time and doth not err.
> Peace far and near; peace to ourselves and her:
> Her body is at peace in holy ground,
> Her spirit is at peace where Angels kneel.

Where sunless rivers weep
  Their waves into the deep,
She sleeps a charmed sleep:
Awake her not.
Led by a single star,
She came from very far
To seek where shadows are
Her pleasant lot.

She left the rosy morn,
She left the fields of corn,
For twilight cold and lorn
And water springs.
Through sleep, as through a veil,
She sees the sky look pale,
And hears the nightingale
That sadly sings.

Rest, rest, a perfect rest
Shed over brow and breast;
Her face is toward the west,
The purple land.
She cannot see the grain
Ripening on hill and plain;
She cannot feel the rain
Upon her hand.

Rest, rest, for evermore
Upon a mossy shore;
Rest, rest at the heart's core
Till time shall cease:
Sleep that no pain shall wake;
Night that no morn shall break
Till joy shall overtake
Her perfect peace.

37 CHRISTINA ROSSETTI, 'SWEET DEATH' 1849

Here is another poem by Christina Rossetti extolling death, and it is not the last such that will appear in this anthology. It is tempting to stereotype her as a reclusive sickly Victorian spinster who looked forward to death as a welcome exit from a miserable and cramped existence. In fact, she led an active life committed to philanthropic causes, and the strong focus on death in her poetry should not be taken as indicating a morbid imagination.

In her recent biography[19] Emma Mason has underlined Rossetti's commitment to ecology and her strong interest in the cycle of nature whereby death is an essential precursor to new life. She requested a natural burial in a wicker coffin so that her own body could disintegrate into and fertilize the earth.

Her strong ecological sense informs this poem, written at the age of 19, which presents the thoughts of someone walking through a graveyard on the way to church. Struck by the way the flowers on the graves die and fall 'to nourish the rich earth', she is led to reflect on how life is sweet but death is sweeter, turning all colours to green, and on how the permanence and truth of God surpass worldly preoccupations like youth and beauty. The 'full harvest' of death is preferable to the meagre yield of earthly crops as represented by Ruth's gleanings of what was left over at the edge of fields described in the Old Testament. This last image is recalled in Edith Sitwell's poem 'Eurydice' in the lines 'Love is not changed by Death, and nothing is lost and all in the end is harvest.'

The process of recycling in nature, with life coming out of death, is a major theme in mid-nineteenth-century poetry. In 'All Nature Has a Feeling' (1845) John Clare writes that 'woods, fields and brooks are life eternal' and immortal because 'their decay is the green life of change; to pass away and come again in blooms revivified'. Walt Whitman's 'This Compost' (1856) marvels at the way that the earth, full as it is with 'distemper'd corpses' and 'work'd over with sour dead' yet 'grows such sweet things out of such corruptions'.

19 *Christina Rossetti: Poetry, Ecology, Faith* (Oxford: OUP, 2018).

The sweetest blossoms die.
  And so it was that, going day by day
Unto the church to praise and pray,
And crossing the green churchyard thoughtfully,
I saw how on the graves the flowers
Shed their fresh leaves in showers,
And how their perfume rose up to the sky
Before it passed away.

The youngest blossoms die.
They die, and fall and nourish the rich earth
From which they lately had their birth;
Sweet life, but sweeter death that passeth by
And is as though it had not been: —
All colours turn to green:
The bright hues vanish, and the odours fly,
The grass hath lasting worth.

And youth and beauty die.
So be it, O my God, Thou God of truth:
Better than beauty and than youth
Are Saints and Angels, a glad company;
And Thou, O Lord, our Rest and Ease,
Are better far than these.
Why should we shrink from our full harvest? Why
Prefer to glean with Ruth?

38 John Ellerton, 'God of the Living' 1858

John Ellerton (1826–1893) was one of the most pastorally minded Victorian clergymen. He spent much of his ministry as vicar of Crewe Green in Cheshire. While there, he wrote eighty-six hymns, including the one for which he is best remembered today, 'The day Thou gavest, Lord, is ended'. He is said to have composed them while walking to and from the Mechanics' Institute, where he taught evening classes.

This particular hymn emphatically asserts that no souls are lost to God and that the dead live on perpetually in the divine embrace. It reminds me of the idea articulated by the distinguished theoretical physicist and Anglican priest John Polkinghorne that life beyond death involves us being held in God's memory.

The universalist implications of the hymn disturbed the proprietors of *Hymns Ancient and Modern*, who asked the author to put more emphasis on judgement and election. Ellerton refused, writing:

> I do not *deny* Hell, or *assert* Purgatory; I merely say that the soul which departs from the body does not depart from the range of God's love. Surely it is recalling the worst side of doctrinal Calvinism to assert this only of those few whom we can honestly call faithful Christians. The belief that *all live with Him* is the only belief which can justify the Church in expressing hope in the Burial Service over all whatsoever their lives who are not formally excommunicate. Most of our funeral hymns either presuppose that the deceased was an eminent saint, or else say nothing which can give hope and comfort to mourners at the very moment when their hearts are most ready to receive the gospel of God's love ... If you think it wise to withdraw all suggestion of the possibility of mercy in the future life of the great mass of the parishioners, it would I think be better for you to cancel the hymn ... I cannot alter it without destroying it.

Other hymnbooks have included Ellerton's hymn. I managed to get it into the current (fourth) edition of the Church of Scotland's *Church Hymnary*. It would be good to hear it sung in funeral services. It goes well to J. B. Dykes' tune Melita.

God of the living, in whose eyes
Unveiled thy whole creation lies,
All souls are thine; we must not say
That those are dead who pass away,
From this our world of flesh set free;
We know them living unto thee.

Released from earthly toil and strife,
With thee is hidden still their life;
Thine are their thoughts, their works, their powers,
All thine, and yet most truly ours,
For well we know, where'er they be,
Our dead are living unto thee.

Not spilt like water on the ground,
Not wrapped in dreamless sleep profound,
Not wandering in unknown despair
Beyond thy voice, thine arm, thy care;
Not left to lie like fallen tree;
Not dead, but living unto thee.

Thy word is true, thy will is just;
To thee we leave them, Lord, in trust;
And bless thee for the love which gave
Thy Son to fill a human grave,
That none might fear that world to see
Where all are living unto thee.

39 ADELAIDE ANNE PROCTER, 'THE BEAUTIFUL ANGEL, DEATH'
1858

Adelaide Anne Procter (1825–1864) was the second most popular Victorian poet after Alfred Tennyson. A convert to Roman Catholicism, she was heavily involved in charitable work on behalf of the homeless and was a pioneer feminist. She had poor health throughout her life and died of tuberculosis at the age of 38.

Many of her poems eagerly look forward to heaven for the escape that it will bring from the 'fierce pain and pleasures dim' of this world. This one is typical, both in singling out children, at a time when infant mortality was high, and also in confidently affirming that God will 'give us back those who are gone before'.

The angel of death features as a benign and welcoming presence in many of Procter's poems, most famously in the form of 'Death's bright angel' in 'The Lost Chord', which in Sir Arthur Sullivan's setting became the best-selling parlour ballad in the last quarter of the nineteenth century. Rumi also enthusiastically embraced this figure, writing that 'the angel of death arrives and I spring joyfully up'. Christina Rossetti's poems about heaven are similarly filled with images of angels.

Adelaide Procter's enthusiastic embrace of death surely speaks especially powerfully to those, like her, who have endured much physical pain and are finding life increasingly weary and burdensome. In another of her poems a father, asked by his son what life is, answers that it is 'a battle, where the strongest lance may fail, where the wariest eyes may be beguiled and the stoutest heart may quail'. The dialogue continues:

'What is Death, Father?'
'The rest, my child,
When the strife and the toil are o'er;
The Angel of God, who, calm and mild,
Says we need fight no more;
Who, driving away the demon band,
Bids the din of the battle cease;
Takes banner and spear from our failing hand,
And proclaims an eternal Peace.'

Why shouldst thou fear the beautiful angel, Death,
      Who waits thee at the portals of the skies,
Ready to kiss away thy struggling breath,
Ready with gentle hand to close thine eyes?

How many a tranquil soul has passed away,
Fled gladly from fierce pain and pleasures dim,
To the eternal splendour of the day;
And many a troubled heart still calls for him.

Spirits too tender for the battle here
Have turned from life, its hopes, its fears, its charms;
And children, shuddering at a world so drear,
Have smiling passed away into his arms.

He whom thou fearest will, to ease its pain,
Lay his cold hand upon thy aching heart:
Will soothe the terrors of thy troubled brain,
And bid the shadow of earth's grief depart.

He will give back what neither time, nor might,
Nor passionate prayer, nor longing hope restore.
(Dear as to long blind eyes recovered sight,)
He will give back those who are gone before.

Oh, what were life, if life were all? Thine eyes
Are blinded by their tears, or thou wouldst see
Thy treasures wait thee in the far-off skies,
And Death, thy friend, will give them all to thee.

40 ADELAIDE ANNE PROCTER, 'A LITTLE LONGER'
1858

Some readers may have had enough of Adelaide Procter's positive courting of death, finding it dangerously maudlin and morbid.

It is by no means to everyone's taste, but I share two more of her poems here in the hope that they may speak to and help those who find themselves wearying of the pain and discomfort that they are suffering and who feel ready and even impatient to die. The one printed opposite assures them that they will not have to wait long and that their patience will be amply rewarded by the coming joys of heaven, which will make our joys in this life seem pale in comparison.

Adelaide Procter paints a picture of heaven filled with angels, archangels and saints and contrasts the true immortal life to our own shadowy existence here on earth. She welcomes death as a friend, a theme brought out in another of her poems, 'A Tryst with Death'.

I am footsore and very weary,
But I travel to meet a Friend:
The way is long and dreary,
But I know that it soon must end.

He is travelling fast like the whirlwind,
And though I creep slowly on,
We are drawing nearer, nearer,
And the journey is almost done.

I will not fear at his coming,
Although I must meet him alone;
He will look in my eyes so gently,
And take my hand in his own.

Like a dream all my toil will vanish,
When I lay my head on his breast –
But the journey is very weary,
And he only can give me rest!

A little longer still – Patience, Belovèd:
A little longer still, ere Heaven unroll
The Glory, and the Brightness, and the wonder,
Eternal, and divine, that waits thy Soul!

A little longer ere Life true, immortal,
(Not this our shadowy Life,) will be thine own;
And thou shalt stand where winged Archangels worship,
And trembling bow before the Great White Throne.

A little longer still, and Heaven awaits thee,
And fills thy spirit with a great delight;
Then our pale joys will seem a dream forgotten,
Our Sun a darkness, and our Day a Night.

A little longer, and thy Heart, Belovèd,
Shall beat for ever with a Love divine;
And joy so pure, so mighty, so eternal,
No creature knows and lives, will then be thine.

A little longer yet – and angel voices
Shall ring in heavenly chant upon thine ear;
Angels and Saints await thee, and God needs thee:
Beloved, can we bid thee linger here!

41 ARTHUR CLOUGH, 'THE STREAM OF LIFE' 1858

Arthur Hugh Clough (1819–1861) is perhaps the supreme exemplar of the Victorian crisis of faith. Having resigned his Oxford fellowship because he felt that he could no longer in conscience subscribe to the teachings and articles of the Church of England, he became a leading apostle of honest doubt, wrestling in his poems with questions of faith and belief.

This poem makes the familiar analogy between a stream descending to the sea and life descending to death. What distinguishes Clough's contribution is his honest uncertainty about whether there is an afterlife, expressed in the last two verses. The roar that he hears upon the shore brings to mind the 'melancholy, long, withdrawing roar' of the once full sea of faith in the poem 'Dover Beach' by his contemporary, Matthew Arnold.

Like another contemporary, Alfred Tennyson, writing about death and what may lie beyond it in 'In Memoriam', Clough falters where he once firmly trod and feels that all he can do is to 'faintly trust the larger hope' and perhaps divine 'a sun will shine and be above us still'. Another of his poems, which also employs the image of the sea, does suggest a rather greater measure of faith.

That there are powers above us I admit;
It may be true too
That while we walk the troublous tossing sea,
That when we see the o'ertopping waves advance,
And when we feel our feet beneath us sink,
There are who walk beside us; and the cry
That rises so spontaneous to the lips,
The 'Help us or we perish' is not nought,
An evanescent spectrum of disease.
It may be that in deed and not in fancy
A hand that is not ours upstays our steps,
A voice that is not ours commands the waves,
Commands the waves, and whispers in our ear
O thou of little faith, why didst thou doubt?
That there are beings above us I believe.

O stream descending to the sea,
   Thy mossy banks between,
The flow'rets blow, the grasses grow,
   The leafy trees are green.

In garden plots the children play,
   The fields the labourers till,
And houses stand on either hand,
   And thou descendest still.

O life descending into death,
   Our waking eyes behold,
Parent and friend thy lapse attend,
   Companions young and old.

Strong purposes our mind possess,
   Our hearts affections fill,
We toil and earn, we seek and learn,
   And thou descendest still.

O end to which our currents tend,
   Inevitable sea,
To which we flow, what do we know,
   What shall we guess of thee?

A roar we hear upon thy shore,
   As we our course fulfil;
Scarce we divine a sun will shine
   and be above us still.

42 F. D. MAURICE ON HEAVEN
1861

Frederick Denison Maurice (1805–1872) grew up as a Unitarian and retained many of the characteristic beliefs of that most liberal and open-minded branch of Christianity even though he spent more than half of his life as an Anglican priest. His career was not without controversy – he was dismissed from his professorship at King's College, London, for denying the doctrine of eternal punishment and supporting Christian socialism. However, he lived to see his views about the afterlife become widely accepted and mainstream, not least within the Church of England.

Maurice's view of heaven, as presented opposite in lectures he gave in 1861 on the Book of Revelation, stands in marked contrast to the sentimental and static picture of angelic choruses endlessly strumming harps and singing hymns of praise presented in popular tracts, verses and sermons. For him, as for the American Unitarian preacher William Channing (**34**), heaven is a state of strenuous activity, reconciliation and progressive development in which one can 'complete tasks which death will leave unfinished, recover affections which have been broken, know what you have been unable to know, work bravely and rest without ceasing to work'. There is room in its many mansions for every form of life.

For Maurice, the key to understanding the concept of eternal life is to detach it from any notion of time. Eternity is better expressed by a circle than by a line, being a quality of experience rather than a matter of temporal duration. To know God and to dwell in Christ is to experience eternal life and to live in heaven now, just as self-imposed separation from God is eternal death. Although he vehemently denied that he was a Universalist, and maintained that eternal loss is a real possibility for those who consciously reject fellowship with God in Christ, his teaching about the depth and breadth of God's love and profound distaste for hellfire preaching bring him very close to espousing a belief in universal salvation. While he insisted that heaven was a state of being, not a place, his view of it as an extension of life on earth was highly influential in helping to create the widespread Victorian belief that death would be like a homecoming with friends reunited and familiar tasks awaiting.

Oftentimes it has been said in Christian pulpits, that heaven is but the continuance of the worship upon earth. Those who have found that worship on earth very dreary and unsatisfactory have said that they would prefer any Greek Elysium or Gothic Valhalla to such a heaven. I think if we take St John as our guide – if we accept his revelation as the true revelation – we may see a meaning in the assertion of the divine, and a meaning in the protest of the layman. All is worship there, because all are pursuing the highest good in contemplation and action; because all are referring their thoughts and acts to one centre, instead of scattering and dispersing them by turning to a thousand different centres; because each thinker and each doer is forgetting himself in the object which she has before him, in the work which is committed to him.

The heavenly worship is continuous only because growth in knowledge is continuous, and because all free action is continuous. In the many mansions there is room for every form of life, only the shapes of death can be excluded.

I say, then, we have here the Christian Elysium, or Valhalla, or Paradise, that which you are all looking for when your thoughts are calmest and truest; when you are most tormented by the discords of the world around you, and of your own hearts; when you are most sure there must be a harmony without discords; when you long for scope to complete tasks which death will leave unfinished; when you wish to recover affections which have been broken; to know what you have been unable to know; to work bravely; to rest without ceasing to work.

43 ROBERT LOWRY, 'THE BEAUTIFUL RIVER' 1864

The inclusion of this gospel song in my *Penguin Book of Hymns* caused some surprise among those who felt it was too slight to warrant a place in such a collection. I believe that it has considerable pastoral value and I have sung it at the bedside of a dying friend. It is the very simplicity of both the words and tune which make it so powerful.

Robert Lowry (1826–1899) served as a Baptist pastor in Pennsylvania and New York and wrote the words and music of many gospel songs and hymns. The words of this one came to him as he was sitting in his study in Brooklyn one sultry July afternoon. An epidemic was raging through the city and he found himself pondering the question 'Why do hymn writers say so much about the river of death and so little about the pure river of the water of life?' He wrote the words in fifteen minutes and then sat down at his parlour organ to work out the tune.

The song is based on Revelation 22:1: 'He showed me a pure river of water of life, clear as crystal, proceeding out of the throne of God' (**10**). Lowry delightfully develops this image of heaven to portray us gathering at the river where angel feet have trod and the saints lift their songs of saving grace. When we reach its smiling and shining waters our pilgrimage will cease and we can lay our burdens down. It could not be a more different image from that of the deep and frightening river of death which Christian and Hopeful have to cross to reach the Celestial City in *The Pilgrim's Progress* (**29**), but it is just as biblically authentic.

A hymn written around the same time by Lowry's near contemporary De Witt Huntington (1830–1912), a minister in the US Methodist Episcopal Church, uses similar imagery to portray heaven as home:

> O think of the home over there,
> By the side of the river of light,
> Where the saints, all immortal and fair,
> Are robed in their garments of white.
>
> I'll soon be at home over there,
> For the end of the journey I see;
> Many dear to my heart over there
> Are watching and waiting for me.

Shall we gather at the river,
Where bright angel feet have trod;
With its crystal tide forever
Flowing by the throne of God?

Yes, we'll gather at the river,
The beautiful, the beautiful river;
Gather with the saints at the river
That flows by the throne of God.

On the margin of the river,
Washing up its silver spray,
We will walk and worship ever,
All the happy golden day.

Ere we reach the shining river,
Lay we ev'ry burden down;
Grace our spirits will deliver,
And provide a robe and crown.

At the smiling of the river,
Mirror of the Saviour's face,
Saints whom death will never sever,
Lift their songs of saving grace.

Soon we'll reach the shining river,
Soon our pilgrimage will cease;
Soon our happy hearts will quiver
With the melody of peace.

44 MARY EMILY BRADLEY, 'IN DEATH'
1865

Mary Emily Bradley, née Neely (1835–1898), was born in Maryland, lived most of her life in New York, and wrote one volume of poetry and a number of stories for girls. She warrants a place in this anthology for the arresting poem opposite in which she imagines herself as someone who has just died, leaving the sobbing voices of those gathered around her and her own desperate struggle for breath to enter a place of perfect peace and utter rest. As for Adelaide Anne Procter, death for her is a state of 'boundless bliss' and 'loveliness' and she realizes how foolish she was ever to have feared it. Indeed, she goes so far as to reflect in the closing line that if the world knew how lovely death is, 'the world would cease to be'.

Mary Bradley wrote another poem about death in which she took up an image that was popular with a number of nineteenth-century writers seeking to describe the idea of resurrection and new life coming out of death. It tells of a delicate little girl finding something the like of which she has never seen before. She is not sure whether it is alive or dead. Her mother tells her that it is a chrysalis and explains:

> How, slowly, in the dull brown thing
> Now still as death, a spotted wing,
> And then another, would unfold,
> Till from the empty shell would fly
> A pretty creature, by and by,
> All radiant in blue and gold.

Tragically, the girl dies before the chrysalis hatches out.

> Today the butterfly has flown,
> She was not here to see it fly,
> And sorrowing I wonder why
> The empty shell is mine alone.
> Perhaps the secret lies in this:
> I too had found a chrysalis,
> And Death that robbed me of delight
> Was but the radiant creature's flight!

How still the room is! But a while ago
The sound of sobbing voices vexed my ears,
And on my face there fell a rain of tears –
I scarce knew why or whence, but now I know.
For this sweet speaking silence, this surcease
Of the dumb, desperate struggle after breath,
This painless consciousness of perfect peace,
Which fills the place of anguish – it is Death!
What folly to have feared it! Not the best
Of all we knew of life can equal this,
Blending in one the sense of utter rest,
The vivid certainty of boundless bliss!
O Death, the loveliness that is in thee,
Could the world know, the world would cease to be.

45 JOHN HENRY NEWMAN, *THE DREAM OF GERONTIUS*
1865

*T*he *Dream of Gerontius* provides one of the most powerful descriptions of death and its immediate aftermath in all Christian literature, at once both disturbing and consoling. Its spiritual and emotional impact is considerably enhanced by Edward Elgar's sublime musical setting. John Henry Newman wrote it twenty years after being received into the Roman Catholic church at a time when he was seized with a sense of his own mortality, possibly as a result of the stroke suffered by his good friend John Keble. The Catholic doctrine of purgatory, the intermediate state after death where souls are purified and fitted for heaven, is prominent in the poem.

The extract opposite comes from the beginning of the second part of the poem when Gerontius, conceived as Everyman, has just died, having been sent on his way out of the world by the prayer of commendation offered at his deathbed by the priest whose ever-more-distant voice he hears as in a dream. He describes feeling an inexpressive lightness and sense of freedom along with a silence and deep rest, which has something of sternness and pain as well as being soothing and sweet.

This ambiguity continues to characterize his post-mortem experience as his soul is led by the angel who greets him on the other side to the judgement court, where he is assailed by a chorus of demons seeking to gather souls for hell. The Angel of Agony pleads his cause, invoking the double agony undergone by Christ in the garden of Gethsemane and on the cross of Calvary, and he is also helped through the ordeal of judgement by the prayers of the priest and the friends, whose voices he hears again. His ransomed soul is lowered into the 'penal waters' of purgatory, enfolded in the loving arms of an angel who promises that other angels will tend and nurse him, and leaves him with these words:

> *Farewell but not forever! brother dear,*
> *Be brave and patient on thy bed of sorrow;*
> *Swiftly shall pass the night of trial here,*
> *And I will come and wake thee on the morrow.*

I went to sleep; and now I am refreshed.
A strange refreshment for I feel in me
An inexpressive lightness, and a sense
Of freedom, as I were at length myself,
And ne'er had been before. How still it is!
I hear no more the busy beat of time,
No, nor my fluttering breath, nor struggling pulse;
Nor does one moment differ from the next.
I had a dream; yes – some one softly said
'He's gone'; and then a sigh went round the room.
And then I surely heard a priestly voice
Cry 'Subvenite'; and they knelt in prayer.
I seem to hear him still; but thin and low,
And fainter and more faint the accents come,
As at an ever-widening interval.
Ah! whence is this? What is this severance?
This silence pours a solitariness
Into the very essence of my soul:
And the deep rest so soothing and so sweet
Hath something too of sternness and of pain ...
So much I know, not knowing how I know,
That the vast universe, where I have dwelt,
Is quitting me, or I am quitting it ...

Another marvel: some one has me fast
Within his ample palm; 'tis not a grasp
Such as they use on earth, but all around
Over the surface of my subtle being,
As though I were a sphere, and capable
To be accosted thus, a uniform
And gentle pressure tells me I am not
Self-moving, but borne forward on my way.
And hark! I hear a singing; yet in sooth
I cannot of that music rightly say
Whether I hear, or touch, or taste the tones.
Oh, what a heart-subduing melody!

46 JOHN GREENLEAF WHITTIER, 'THE ETERNAL GOODNESS'
1865

John Greenleaf Whittier (1807–1892), an American Quaker who was a member of the Massachusetts state legislature and a prolific poet, is best known as the author of the hymn 'Dear Lord and Father of Mankind'.

In 'The Eternal Goodness' he expresses his uncertainty about what will happen to us after death, but holds firm in his faith that we will never drift beyond God's love and care. His description of waiting on the shore beside the silent sea for the 'muffled oar' which signals death conjures up an image that has been employed at least since the time of the ancient Greeks with the figure of Charon ferrying souls across the Styx to Hades. When the travel writer and journalist Jan Morris died in 2020, her son said that she had begun 'her greatest journey, leaving behind on the shore her life-long partner, Elizabeth'.

The image of death as a silent sea (although in this case without a shore) recurs in a poem which Reynold Nicholson wrote to express what he saw as the philosophy of the Persian mystic Rumi (**17** and **18**):

> *Deep in our hearts the light of heaven is shining*
> *Upon a soundless sea without a shore,*
> *Oh, happy they who found it in resigning*
> *The images of all that men adore.*

The reference in the last verse of Whittier's poem to islands lifting 'their fronded palms in air' harks back to the belief in isles of the blessed located in far-off oceans as abodes of the dead, which we have already noted in Plato and the Brendan voyage (**4** and **15**).

For all its poetic imagery, the message of this poem is a very simple one, echoing St Paul's words in Romans 8:38 that in the words of the New Living Translation: 'Neither death nor life, neither angels nor demons, neither our fears for today nor our worries about tomorrow – not even the powers of hell can separate us from God's love.'

I long for household voices gone,
For vanished smiles I long,
But God hath led my dear ones on,
And He can do no wrong.

I know not what the future hath
Of marvel or surprise,
Assured alone that life and death
His mercy underlies.

And if my heart and flesh are weak
To bear an untried pain,
The bruised reed He will not break,
But strengthen and sustain.

No offering of my own I have,
Nor works my faith to prove;
I can but give the gifts He gave,
And plead His love for love.

And so beside the Silent Sea
I wait the muffled oar;
No harm from Him can come to me
On ocean or on shore.

I know not where His islands lift
Their fronded palms in air;
I only know I cannot drift
Beyond His love and care.

47 CHRISTINA ROSSETTI ON RIVERS RUNNING TO THE SEA
1865–1892

These three extracts provide rather beautiful evocations of death as a river running into the sea, a popular theme of Christina Rossetti's poetry, which we have already encountered in the lines 'her life is lapsing like a stream that makes no noise but floweth on apace seawards' in her sonnet 'Life Hidden' (see **36**).

The first extract opposite includes the same phrase, 'the inevitable sea', that Arthur Hugh Clough uses in 'The Stream of Life' (**41**). The second emphasizes the theme of seeking rather than flowing, also found in this poem by Rossetti's exact contemporary, Emily Dickinson:

My river runs to thee –
Blue Sea! Wilt welcome me?
My river waits reply –
Oh Sea – look graciously –
I'll fetch thee brooks
From spotted nooks –
Say – Sea – Take me!

The third extract is part of a devotional meditation on the Book of Revelation entitled 'The Face of the Deep' written shortly before Christina Rossetti's death in 1892. It conveys a wonderful sense of our own waters mingling with those of God's shoreless sea. There are echoes here of Shelley's poem 'Love's Philosophy' (1819), about intimate human relationships:

The fountains mingle with the river
And the rivers with the ocean,
The winds of heaven mix forever
With a sweet emotion;
Nothing in the world is single,
All things by a law divine
In another's being mingle –
Why not I with thine?

L ife flows down to death; we cannot bind
 That current that it should not flee:
Life flows down to death, as rivers find
The inevitable sea.

                            from 'An Immatura Sister'

A s rivers seek the sea,
 Much more deep than they,
So my soul seeks thee
Far away.

                            from 'Confluences'

L ord, we are rivers running to Thy sea,
 Our waves and ripples all derived from Thee:
A nothing we should have, a nothing be,
Except for Thee.
Sweet are the waters of Thy shoreless sea,
Make sweet our waters that make haste to Thee;
Pour in Thy sweetness, that ourselves may be
Sweetness to Thee.

                            from 'Christ is our All in All'

48 John Ellerton, 'Now the Labourer's Task Is O'er' 1870

Here is another wonderfully pastoral funeral hymn by John Ellerton. No one could fault its orthodoxy in terms of its clear statement of the Christian doctrine of the post-mortem state as being one akin to sleep with the individual soul being judged and the hope of an eventual day of general resurrection. This doctrinal teaching is infused and overlaid with an overwhelming sense of divine mercy.

The hymn begins with the familiar image of the voyager landing 'upon the farther shore' and entering into a restful sleep with his labours and battles on earth over. We are assured that in death the tears of earth are dried, hidden things will be made clear and our lives will be judged by 'a juster judge than here'. This comforting message is confirmed by reference to the Parable of the Good Shepherd bringing home the lost sheep to the shelter of the fold and to sinful souls turning their dying eyes to the cross of Christ. There is an allusion in the penultimate verse to Jesus' descent into hell after his own death to release the souls trapped there. Although not explicitly stated in the Bible, this is hinted at in verses in the first Epistle of Peter and the Letter to the Ephesians and expressed in the line in the Apostles' Creed 'He descended into Hell'. The belief being expressed here is that Jesus himself went through the experience not just of dying but of being dead. His soul joined those already dead in order to bring them with him into eternal life.

Similar sentiments are expressed in another wonderful Victorian hymn written by Frederick William Faber:

> *There's a wideness in God's mercy,*
> *like the wideness of the sea;*
> *there's a kindness in his justice*
> *which is more than liberty.*
>
> *There is no place where earth's sorrows*
> *are more felt than up in heaven:*
> *there is no place where earth's failings*
> *have such kindly judgement given.*

Now the labourer's task is o'er;
Now the battle day is past;
Now upon the farther shore
Lands the voyager at last.

Father, in Thy gracious keeping
Leave we now Thy servant sleeping.

There the tears of earth are dried;
There its hidden things are clear;
There the work of life is tried
By a juster Judge than here.

There the Shepherd, bringing home
Many a lamb forlorn and strayed,
Shelters each, no more to roam,
Where the wolf can ne'er invade.

There the sinful souls, that turn
To the cross their dying eyes,
All the love of Christ shall learn
At His feet in Paradise.

There no more the powers of hell
Can prevail to mar their peace;
Christ the Lord shall guard them well,
He Who died for their release.

'Earth to earth, and dust to dust,'
Calmly now the words we say;
Left behind, we wait in trust
For the resurrection day.

49 CARMINA GADELICA, THE DEATH DIRGE
1870s

This rather beautiful dirge to be sung over someone who is dying, with its strong emphasis on sleep and on going home, is one of several similar Gaelic prayers and poems collected in the islands of the Outer Hebrides by Alexander Carmichael (1832–1912) and published in English in his *Carmina Gadelica*. A moving description which he gives of these death blessings suggests that the figure of the *anamchara*, or soul friend, familiar in early Celtic Christianity, had developed into a specialized form of lay ministry to the dying and was still very much in existence in the Hebrides in the late nineteenth century:

> Death blessings vary in words but not in spirit. They are known by various names, such as Death Blessing, Soul Leading, Soul Peace, and others familiar to the people.
>
> The soul peace is intoned, not necessarily by a cleric, over the dying, and the man or the woman who says it is called *anam-chara* (soul friend). He or she is held in special affection by the friends of the dying person ever after. The soul peace is slowly sung – all present earnestly joining the soul friend in beseeching the Three Persons of the Godhead and all the saints of heaven to receive the departing soul of earth. During the prayer the soul friend makes the sign of the cross with the right thumb over the lips of the dying. The scene is touching and striking in the extreme.[21]

Carmichael notes that the death blessings and soul leadings were pronounced by the *anamchara* with the purpose of speeding the dying person on his or her pilgrimage, which was variously described as being across the black river of death, the great ocean of darkness, or the mountains of eternity. At the moment of death, when 'the soul is seen ascending like a bright ball of light into the clouds', those present join the *anamchara* in saying:

> *The poor soul is now set free*
> *Outside the soul shrine.*

[21]   Alexander Carmichael, *Carmina Gadelica* (Edinburgh: Floris Books, 1992), p.578.

Thou goest home this night to thy home of winter,
To thy home of autumn, of spring, and of summer;
Thou goest home this night to thy perpetual home,
To thine eternal bed, to thine eternal slumber.

Sleep thou, sleep, and away with thy sorrow,
Sleep thou, sleep, and away with thy sorrow,
Sleep thou, sleep, and away with thy sorrow;
Sleep, thou beloved, in the Rock of the fold.

Sleep this night in the breast of thy Mother,
Sleep, thou beloved, while she herself soothes thee;
Sleep thou this night on the Virgin's arm,
Sleep, thou beloved, while she herself kisses thee.

The great sleep of Jesus, the surpassing sleep of Jesus,
The sleep of Jesus' wound, the sleep of Jesus' grief.
The young sleep of Jesus, the restoring sleep of Jesus,
The sleep of the kiss of Jesus of peace and of glory.

The sleep of the seven lights be thine, beloved,
The sleep of the seven joys be thine, beloved,
The sleep of the seven slumbers be thine, beloved,
On the arm of the Jesus of blessings, the Christ of grace.

The shade of death lies upon thy face, beloved,
But the Jesus of grace has His hand round about thee,
In nearness to the Trinity farewell to thy pains,
Christ stands before thee and peace is in this mind.

Sleep, O sleep in the calm of all calm,
Sleep, O sleep in the guidance of guidance,
Sleep, O sleep in the love of all love,
Sleep, O beloved, in the Lord of life,
Sleep, O beloved, in the God of life.

50 TWO SPIRITUALS ABOUT CROSSING THE RIVER JORDAN
1875

'Swing Low, Sweet Chariot' and 'Deep River' are two of the best-known and best-loved African American spirituals. They portray death as a homecoming, with friends being reunited, welcomed by angels and given crowns to wear at the gospel feast. What is particularly striking in both is the focus on crossing the river Jordan, a theme which recurs in many spirituals, such as

> One more river
> And that's the river of Jordan,
> One more river,
> There's one more river to cross.
>
> I'll meet you in the morning
> When you reach the promised land
> On the other side of the Jordan
> For I'm bound for the promised land.

While these songs are primarily about crossing the river between life and death, and so bringing liberation to those enslaved in the cotton plantations where they were composed and first sung, there are other resonances in their references to the river Jordan. Wide American rivers, notably the Red river, which forms the boundary between Texas and Oklahoma before flowing through Arkansas and Louisiana, were formidable barriers to freedom for escaping slaves seeking to reach the 'promised land' of the free states which had abolished slavery.

'Swing Low, Sweet Chariot', which was written by Wallace Willis, a freed slave, draws its inspiration from the story of Elijah being taken up to heaven in a chariot in 2 Kings 2. The reference to 'campground' in 'Deep River' is almost certainly to the camp meetings, usually overtly Christian gatherings, illegal in some areas, where slaves could meet, sing, tell stories, and share their sorrows and hopes. Here, too, there is a double meaning with the 'campground' also being conceived as heaven, the place where all will be truly set free.

Swing low, sweet chariot,
Coming for to carry me home.
Swing low, sweet chariot;
Coming for to carry me home
I looked over Jordan and what did I see
Coming for to carry me home?
A band of angels coming after me,
Coming for to carry me home.
If you get there before I do,
Coming for to carry me home,
Tell all my friends I'm coming, too,
Coming for to carry me home.

Deep River, my home is over Jordan.
Deep River, Lord, I want to cross over into campground.
Oh, don't you want to go to that gospel feast;
That promised land where all is peace?
Walk into heaven and take my seat,
and cast my crown at Jesus' feet.
Oh, when I get to heav'n, I walk all about,
There's nobody there for to turn me out.
Deep River, my home is over Jordan.
Deep River, Lord, I want to cross over into campground.

51 WILLIAM ERNEST HENLEY, 'IN MEMORIAM R. G. C. B.'
1878

William Ernest Henley (1849–1903) was a leading literary figure in the last decade of the nineteenth century. Afflicted with excruciatingly painful tuberculosis of the bone, he spent two years in hospital in his mid-twenties, had his left leg amputated below the knee and only narrowly avoided amputation of his right leg. With his wooden stump and crutch, he provided his close friend Robert Louis Stevenson with the inspiration for the character of Long John Silver in *Treasure Island*.

Henley faced his painful illness with stoical resolve. Towards the end of his time in hospital he wrote the poem for which he is best remembered and which came to be known as 'Invictus'. It ends with the affirmation 'I am the master of my fate: I am the captain of my soul'. Although not possessed of a conventional religious faith, he had a strong sense that there was a power that shaped the universe and that death provided an ultimate and positive destination for humanity. His own death came at the age of 53 after a fall from a moving railway carriage brought about a recurrence of his tuberculosis.

It was perhaps the considerable suffering and adversity that he experienced that contributed to Henley's very positive view of death, as expressed in another of his poems:

> *From the winter's grey despair,*
> *From the summer's golden languor,*
> *Death, the lover of life,*
> *Frees us for ever.*

In the poem opposite, written in memory of a friend identified only by his initials, Henley returns to the idea of death as our lover – indeed, the last of our lovers – and comforter. He portrays it as both grave and sweet, glad and sorrowful, but ultimately it is its positive aspect that he emphasizes with his repeated affirmation 'the ways of Death are soothing and serene'.

The ways of Death are soothing and serene,
    And all the words of Death are grave and sweet.
From camp and church, the fireside and the street,
She beckons forth – and strife and song have been.

A summer night descending cool and green
And dark on daytime's dust and stress and heat,
The ways of Death are soothing and serene,
And all the words of Death are grave and sweet.

O glad and sorrowful, with triumphant mien
And radiant faces look upon, and greet
This last of all your lovers, and to meet
Her kiss, the Comforter's, your spirit lean –
The ways of Death are soothing and serene.

52 CHRISTINA ROSSETTI, 'AN OLD-WORLD THICKET'

1881

The verses opposite form the closing portion of a long poem which Christina Rossetti wrote not long after her sister had suffered a particularly painful death and while her brother, the poet and painter Dante Gabriel Rossetti, was terminally ill.

The poem is set in a wood through which the narrator walks, as if in a dream, feeling an increasing sense of death and gloom with 'a universal sound of lamentation' and darkness descending. In these final verses the landscape is suddenly and dramatically transformed to one of warmth, sunshine and brightness. The pattering of feet, the sound of bleating and the tinkling of a bell herald the appearance of a flock of sheep making their way through the trees and journeying westwards towards the setting sun and their rest.

This is clearly an allegory of the peaceful progress of the Christian soul, and indeed of all creation, towards heaven. The patriarchal ram leading the sheep recalls the ram caught by its horns in a thicket which provides the sacrificial victim in the story of Abraham and Isaac in Genesis 22:13 and serves as an archetype for Christ, the lamb slain from the foundation of the world who leads us through repentance to eternal life.

I find this a particularly comforting imagining of our own journeys towards death. There are echoes of Thomas Gray's 'Elegy Written in a Country Churchyard':

> *The curfew tolls the knell of parting day,*
> *The lowing herd wind slowly o'er the lea,*
> *The ploughman homeward plods his weary way,*
> *And leaves the world to darkness and to me.*

But while Gray goes on to focus on human mortality and bodily decay, Rosetti's emphasis is on the peaceful and joyful journey to heaven.

Without, within me, music seemed to be;
    Something not music, yet most musical,
Silence and sound in heavenly harmony;
    At length a pattering fall
Of feet, a bell, and bleatings, broke through all.

Then I looked up. The wood lay in a glow
From golden sunset and from ruddy sky;
The sun had stooped to earth though once so high;
    Had stooped to earth, in slow
Warm dying loveliness brought near and low.

Each twig was tipped with gold, each leaf was edged
And veined with gold from the gold-flooded west;
Each mother-bird, and mate-bird, and unfledged
    Nestling, and curious nest,
Displayed a gilded moss or beak or breast.

And filing peacefully between the trees,
Having the moon behind them, and the sun
Full in their meek mild faces, walked at ease
    A homeward flock, at peace
With one another and with every one.

A patriarchal ram with tinkling bell
Led all his kin; sometimes one browsing sheep
  Hung back a moment, or one lamb would leap
    And frolic in a dell;
Yet still they kept together, journeying well,

And bleating, one or other, many or few,
Journeying together toward the sunlit west;
Mild face by face, and woolly breast by breast,
    Patient, sun-brightened too,
Still journeying toward the sunset and their rest.

53 GEORGE MATHESON, 'O LOVE THAT WILT NOT LET ME GO' 1882

The blind Church of Scotland minister George Matheson (1842–1906) penned this much-loved hymn in his manse in Innellan on the Firth of Clyde when, in his own words, 'something had happened which caused me the most severe mental suffering'.

The image of giving back our weary souls so they may have a richer and fuller life in God's ocean depths echoes the language of many Christian mystics. The fourth-century ascetic Evagrius Ponticus uses the analogy of rivers flowing back to the sea to represent being 'absorbed into God' and regaining lost union with the divine. John Scotus Eriugena (14) describes the divine nature in terms of 'the sea of infinite goodness ready to give itself to those wishing to participate in it'. Meister Eckhart envisages God as 'a sea of infinite substance'. In similar vein, Rumi urges 'Give yourself up without regret and in exchange gain the ocean. In the arms of the sea you will be secure' and Bahá'u'lláh, founder of the Bahá'í faith, asks the 'Lord of all names' to 'lead me unto the ocean of Thy presence'. John Keble's hymn 'Sun of My Soul, Thou Saviour Dear' ends with the lines 'Till in the ocean of thy love, we lose ourselves in heaven above'.

This imagery has many primal resonances. Members of the Wagilak clan of the Ritharrngu Aboriginal Australian peoples believe that each individual's life is a thread woven into a much bigger ongoing string or *raki* into which it is absorbed at death. The souls of the departed are pulled into the deep waters of Blue Mud Bay by a harpoon string as their names are intoned in song. Many near-death experiences involve either floating on or being absorbed into water. For Carl Jung, 'The sea is the container of the unknown and the mysterious'.

The imagery in the second verse of this hymn is explored in the commentary on the next extract (54). Explaining the meaning of its closing lines, Matheson wrote 'I took red as the symbol of that sacrificial life which blooms by shedding itself'. Here is a powerful restatement of the familiar portrayal of death in terms of self-surrender and loss of ego.

O Love that wilt not let me go,
I rest my weary soul in thee;
I give thee back the life I owe,
that in thine ocean depths its flow
may richer, fuller be.

O Light that follow'st all my way,
I yield my flick'ring torch to thee;
my heart restores its borrowed ray,
that in thy sunshine's blaze its day
may brighter, fairer be.

O Joy that seekest me through pain,
I cannot close my heart to thee;
I trace the rainbow thro' the rain,
and feel the promise is not vain
that morn shall tearless be.

O Cross that liftest up my head,
I dare not ask to fly from thee;
I lay in dust life's glory dead,
and from the ground there blossoms red,
life that shall endless be.

54 George Matheson on the Preservation of Personality in Heaven

1884

George Matheson's language in the opening verse of 'O Love That Wilt Not Let Me Go' could be taken as suggesting the disappearance of the individual personality at death as it becomes merged with the infinite like a drop of water dissolving in the sea. In this meditation on the biblical text 'That God may be all in all' (1 Corinthians 15:28), he makes clear that he does not believe that this is what happens. The human personality does not simply melt into the being of God as a cloud melts into the blaze of sunshine. Rather it gains more brightness from being part of God's 'sunshine's blaze' (**53**).

As we have seen, both Eriugena and Rumi liken reabsorption into the divine to stars being overshadowed in the presence of the sun (**14** and **17**). In a meditation entitled 'Does personality survive', Rumi expands on his theme of non-existence in death, explaining that the individual is not annihilated but rather transfigured and deified:

> He exists in respect of the survival of his essence, but his attributes are changed into the attributes of God like the flame of a candle in the presence of the sun. If you put cotton on the flame, the cotton will be consumed; but it gives you no light for the sun has overpowered it.

He also expands on his image of the drop of water in the ocean (**18**), writing 'You are not a drop in the ocean. You are the entire ocean in a drop' and urging 'Plunge into the ocean of consciousness. Let the drop of water that is you become a hundred mighty seas.'

Matheson is more definite about the survival of the individual personality after death but, like Rumi, he emphasizes that it involves an abandonment of the ego: 'the only ocean in which a man loses himself is self-love'. *The Tibetan Book of Living and Dying* puts it like this: 'Think of a wave in the sea. Seen in one way, it seems to have a distinct identity but seen in another it is just part of the water. Every wave is related to every other wave.'

Am I, then, to be lost in God? Is my whole personal life to be absorbed and overshadowed in the life of the Infinite One? Am I to have no more separate being than one of those myriad drops which compose the vast ocean? If so, then my goal is death indeed. If my personality is to melt into the being of God as a cloud melts into the blaze of sunshine, then, surely, is God not my life but my annihilation. He can no longer say of me, 'Because I live, thou shalt live also.'

Nay, but, my soul, thou hast misread the destiny of thy being. It is not merely written that God is to be all, but that He is to be all in all. His universal life is not to destroy the old varieties of being; it is to pulsate through these varieties. His music is to fill the world, but it is to sound through all the varied instruments of the world. His sunshine is to flood the universe, but it is to be mirrored in a thousand various forms. His love is to penetrate creation, but it is to be reflected in the infinite diversities of the hearts and souls of men.

Thou speakest of losing thyself in the ocean of His love, but this is only poetically true. Love is an ocean where no man permanently loses himself; he regains himself in richer, nobler form. The only ocean in which a man loses himself is self-love; God's love gives him back his life that he may keep it unto life eternal.

55 ALFRED TENNYSON, 'CROSSING THE BAR' 1889

For Alfred Tennyson (1809–1892), Poet Laureate through most of Queen Victoria's reign, life after death is 'the cardinal point of Christianity'. It cannot be a matter of absolute certainty, but 'if faith means anything at all, it is trusting to those instincts, or feelings, or whatever they may be called, which assure us of some life after this'.

Tennyson writes most extensively and famously about death and what may lie beyond it in his long poem 'In Memoriam', composed after the death of his great friend Arthur Hallam at the age of 22. I came very close to including an extract from it in this anthology, but it is difficult to express its rich depth and complexity in just a few verses. It is full of questions, of which perhaps the central one is 'How fares it with the happy dead?', but also of hope and trust 'that those we call the dead are breathers of an ampler day for ever nobler ends'.

'Crossing the Bar' was written after Tennyson had experienced a serious illness and was pondering his own mortality. He uses the imagery of crossing over the sandbar to catch the tide where a river meets the sea. Ridges of sand build up around the entrance to harbours and estuaries, keeping the water within them calm. The action of waves over such bars can cause a moaning sound. Living as he did on the Isle of Wight, he was familiar with the strong tides of the Solent and with the arrow-shaped sandbar known as Bramble Bank sited midway between the Hampshire coast and Cowes. Ships traditionally leave harbour as the full tide begins to withdraw.

This poem imagines the dying individual, like a boat, putting out to sea and crossing the bar 'when that which drew from out the boundless deep turns again home'. Borne by the flood from 'our bourne of time and place', the soul, now dead, hopes to see God, 'my Pilot', face to face. Tennyson later wrote 'The Pilot has been on board all the while, but in the dark I have not seen him … [He is] that Divine and Unseen Who is always guiding us.'

Sunset and evening star,
    And one clear call for me!
And may there be no moaning of the bar,
    When I put out to sea,

But such a tide as moving seems asleep,
    Too full for sound and foam,
When that which drew from out the boundless deep
    Turns again home.

Twilight and evening bell,
    And after that the dark!
And may there be no sadness of farewell,
    When I embark;

For tho' from out our bourne of Time and Place
    The flood may bear me far,
I hope to see my Pilot face to face
    When I have crost the bar.

56 W. S. Gilbert,
Death is the Only True Unraveller
1889

This may at first sight seem a curious entry for this anthology. Those who know my writings could be forgiven for concluding that it is only here so that I get in the trademark Gilbert and Sullivan reference that has appeared in almost every one of my forty-plus books. I believe, however, that it points to a profound and important feature of death which is not brought out in any of the other extracts. Death does indeed unravel all the complexities and tangles of our lives.

The observation which W. S. Gilbert (1836–1911) here puts into the mouth of Don Alhambra del Bolero, the Grand Inquisitor of Spain, in his comic opera *The Gondoliers* seems to me to echo in some respects the sentiments of Ecclesiastes 7:29: 'God made us plain and simple but we have made ourselves very complicated.' There does seem to be a human tendency to make our lives unnecessarily complicated. Perhaps true simplicity only comes when the tangled mess that we get ourselves into is unravelled at death. The sixteenth-century Anglican divine Richard Hooker was surely making a somewhat similar point to Gilbert when he said on his deathbed 'I go to a world of order.'

Gilbert had an equivocal attitude to life and death, as exemplified in the ballad he wrote in *The Yeomen of the Guard* which asks 'Is life a boon?' (in which case 'Death, whene'er he call, must call too soon') or 'Is life a thorn?' (in which case 'Then count it not a whit! Man is well done with it'). On the whole, he was in favour of life, even if he took a rather jaundiced view of it. His collaborator in the Savoy operas, Arthur Sullivan, was much more unequivocally a lover of life. The two men expressed their shared philosophy of *carpe diem* (seize the day) in the quintet which follows the Grand Inquisitor's description of death as the only true unraveller. It describes life as a 'pudding full of plums' and 'perhaps the only riddle that we shrink from giving up' and suggests that we should simply 'take it as it comes'.

Life is one closely complicated tangle. Death is the only true unraveller.

57 BENJAMIN JOWETT ON IMMORTALITY
1892

Benjamin Jowett (1817–1893), Anglican clergyman and master of Balliol College, Oxford, with one of the best minds of the Victorian age, wrestled with questions of faith and belief, not least in respect of death and what lay beyond it.

He pondered the subject of immortality in the introduction to his translation of Plato's *Phaedro* (**4**). Observing that 'the doctrine of the immortality of the soul has sunk deep into the heart of the human race', he noted that for most of history it had essentially been a customary rather than a reasoned belief. In his own time, however, scientific advances, including the theory of evolution, the rise of biblical criticism and the waning authority of the church had combined to weaken the hold of the traditional picture of heaven as a place where white-robed angelic choirs surrounded the throne of God.

Jowett grounded his own belief in a future life in philosophical, moral and ethical considerations. First and foremost, he felt that it was consistent with belief in a wise and good God. For him, as for William Channing and F. D. Maurice (**34** and **42**), heaven was not a static state of rest and inactivity. 'The truest conception which we can form of a future life', he wrote,

> is a state of progress or education – a progress from evil to good, from ignorance to knowledge. To this we are led by the analogy of the present life, in which we see different races and nations of men, and different men and women of the same nation, in various states or stages of cultivation.

In imagining what life for the departed might be like, he fell back on some highly traditional and comforting images, such as the idea of coming home and being freed from the cares of the world. Like Maurice, he envisaged the dead continuing the good work they had done on earth and working out God's will 'at a further stage in the heavenly pilgrimage'. He also followed Maurice in viewing immortality not so much as a temporal matter of life everlasting as a state of communion with God, which can occur in this world as in the next. This theme was very much taken up by twentieth-century theologians.

The belief in the immortality of the soul rests at last on the belief in God. If there is a good and wise God, then there is a progress of mankind towards perfection. We cannot suppose that the moral government of God of which we see the beginnings in the world and in ourselves will cease when we pass out of life.

Though we cannot altogether shut out the childish fear that the soul upon leaving the body may 'vanish into thin air', we have still a hope of immortality with which we comfort ourselves on sufficient grounds. The denial of this belief takes the heart out of human life. As Goethe says, 'He is dead even in this world who has no belief in another.'

It is in the language of ideas only that we can speak of the departed. First of all there is the thought of rest and freedom from pain; they have gone home, as the common saying is, and the cares of this world touch them no more. Secondly, we may imagine them as they were at their best and brightest, humbly fulfilling their daily round of duties – selfless, childlike, unaffected by the world; when the eye was single and the whole body seemed to be full of light; when the mind was clear and saw into the purposes of God. Thirdly, we may think of them as possessed by a great love of God and man, working out His will at a further stage in the heavenly pilgrimage. And yet we acknowledge that these are the things which eye hath not seen nor ear heard. Fourthly, there may have been some moments in our own lives when we have risen above ourselves, or been conscious of our truer selves, in which the will of God has superseded our wills, and we have entered into communion with Him, and been partakers for a brief season of the Divine truth and love, in which like Christ we have been inspired to utter the prayer, 'I in them, and thou in me, that we may be all made perfect in one.' These precious moments, if we have ever known them, are the nearest approach we can make to the idea of immortality.

58 George Matheson on the Preparation of Humanity's Dwelling-Place
1895

Here is another wonderfully rich meditation on death by George Matheson inspired by the familiar text of John 14:2: 'In My Father's house are many mansions ... I go to prepare a place for you' (**9**).

Matheson begins by picturing our individual lives moving in a vast sea and seeming to be mere specks amid the waves as we wonder what lies at the end of the universe. For Matheson, what is important is who rather than what awaits us after death. He does not want gorgeous furniture in his Father's house, but rather something homely – 'an old glance of the eye, an old ring of the voice, an old clasp of the hand'. Nor is he bothered by the golden streets, pearly gates and sapphire thrones promised in the Book of Revelation. Rather he wants 'the sympathy of a brother's soul'.

In many ways Matheson is here positing heaven as an extension of life on earth, particularly in its familiar and homely aspects. He is clearly expecting the reuniting of old friends and family. But above all he is comforted by the fact that Jesus has gone there before us to prepare the way. 'I cannot get that place by going over the bridge; I can only get it by someone going over before me. What I want is a heart already there.'

The twentieth-century North American Presbyterian minister and peace activist William Sloane Coffin made a somewhat similar observation before his own death: 'If we don't know what is beyond the grave, we do know who is beyond the grave.'[20] In the final verse of his hymn 'There is a blessed home beyond this land of woe', the nineteenth-century Anglican priest and hymn writer Henry Baker says of the welcome that Jesus gives us in heaven, having gone to prepare a place for us there:

> *Look up, you saints of God, nor fear to tread below*
> *The path your Saviour trod of daily toil and woe:*
> *Wait only for a little while in uncomplaining love.*
> *His own most gracious smile will welcome you above.*

[22] William Sloane Coffin, The Collected Sermons of William Sloane Coffin: The Riverside Years, Volume 1 (Louisville, Kentucky: Westminster John Knox Press, 2008), p. 428.

Often have I been startled by the vastness of that sea in which my little life is moving; I seem but a speck amid myriad waves. I want to know what is at the end of the universe. Is there a human soul there? Is there anything that can respond to my spirit? Is there aught that can love when I love, weep when I weep, joy when I joy? Is there a pulse of sympathy that can answer to the pulse of my heart? Is there a place prepared for me? I cannot get that place by going over the bridge; I can only get it by someone going over before me. What I want is a heart already there, a kindred soul to meet me, a human life to greet me. The 'going before' is itself the 'preparing'.

I want no gorgeous furniture in my room of the Father's house. I am afraid the furniture may be too gorgeous. I want something homely – like home. I seek an old glance of the eye, an old ring of the voice, an old clasp of the hand. I seek the ancient sympathy that has linked man to man, the earthly love that has knit heart to heart, the human trust that has bound life to life. I seek in eternity the image of time; that is the place I would have prepared for me.

Let not thy heart be troubled; in the vast spaces there is a home for thee. The Son of Man has gone before; there is a region prepared for humanity. There is a spot in this stupendous universe where human nature dwells. That spot is thy one comfort, thy one glory. No other glory would make up for it. There may be golden streets and pearly gates and sapphire thrones. There may be rivers clear as crystal, and trees rich in foliage, and flowers full of bloom. There may be suns that never set, and hands that never weary, and lives that never die. But about these many things thy heart is not troubled. One thing is needful, without which all were vain – the sympathy of a brother's soul.

59 GEORGE MATHESON ON THE GROUND FOR SPIRITUAL ANXIETY
1906

In this meditation on the biblical text 'Shall not the day of the Lord be darkness and not light?' (Amos 5:20), written shortly before his own death, George Matheson suggests that there is no need to posit a separate heaven and hell. For the selfish, heaven will be a miserable place. His fear is not that he will be excluded from heaven but rather that because of his own failings he may find it uncongenial: 'I fear to stand by the crystal river and have no eye for its clearness. I dread to walk in the green pastures and have no sense of their richness.' Hence his heartfelt prayer that he may be purged of ego and fitted for rest there.

A similar point is made by Francis Newman, brother of John Henry and a noted freethinker. Despite his doubts, he profoundly respected the Christian view of heaven:

> It has no form or comeliness to the worldly mind, the fierce or hard heart, the meanly ambitious, nor to any who are absorbed in self and contented in sin. Many a scoffer has said of it, 'It is tiresome enough to sing long hymns at church; I should not like at all to be harping and trumpeting day and night on a cloud'. The scoffer does not go on to confess, yet it is nonetheless true, that he has no pleasure in anticipating a land of universal holiness, where every eye looks up with love and joy to the guiding countenance of a righteous Lord. It needs a heart essentially in love with holiness, whatever its sins from bursts of uncontrolled passion, to make the Christian heaven seem desirable …
>
> There is here no vulgar notion of thrones and crowns and sitting on an upper seat, which, scattered here and there in the New Testament, damages the doctrine, and does but gratify ambition; there is no exaltation of self; but, as a mother desires to see the happiness and honour of her son, most unselfishly, so does the spiritual Christian aspire to see the reign of righteousness and holiness triumphant. Faith in such a Paradise seems to me undeniably sanctifying and ennobling.[23][21]

---

[23] F. W. Newman, *On the Vision of Heaven* (Toledo, Index Tracts, 1872), pp. 5–6.

To a selfish man there would be no place in the universe so miserable as heaven. What makes heaven day to Jesus would make it night to Judas – the reign of love. I have been often struck with the question Hosea puts to selfish people: 'What shall ye do in the day of the feast of the Lord?' He does not say they will get no place at the table; he asks what interest they will have in the proceedings when they sit down. How will they appreciate a banquet where every sentiment proposed will be commemorative of sacrifice, and every plaudit raised will be a tribute to the Lamb that was slain! It is not enough to be free from so-called adverse circumstances. The deepest adversity is solitude of soul – the want of harmony with one's environment. It is not enough that I am untouched by the lightning; I must be touched by the sunbeam. I would rather be struck by lightning than struck by nothing, for the soul is dead that slumbers, and the chords that never vibrate are the saddest chords of all.

My father, prepare me for the place of Thy rest! I often speak as if the question were whether Thou wilt let me in. Oh no, that is not, that never was, the question! Thou hast never separated the good and the bad by locality. I doubt not that the wise and foolish virgins entered by the same outward gate; the door that was shut upon the foolish was an inward door. Hast Thou not told me that the man without the wedding garment got in with the white-robed multitude! It was after his entrance that he felt his want. I have no fear that I shall ever be driven from Thy presence; but I wish to enjoy that presence, to bask in it, to sing in it. I fear to stand by the crystal river and have no eye for its clearness. I dread to walk in the green pastures and have no sense of their richness. I am afraid to be at the concert of multitudinous voices and have no ear for their sweetness. I tremble to be enrolled in the league of pity and have no heart for its kindness. Save me, O Father, from an uncongenial heaven!

60 KAHLIL GIBRAN'S *PROPHET* ON DEATH
1923 CE

Born a Maronite Christian in Lebanon, Kahlil Gibran (1883–1931) emigrated to the USA at the age of 12 and spent most of the rest of his life there as a poet and painter. His spiritual writings, which remain very popular, show the influence of Christianity, Islam and Sufi mysticism.

Gibran's *The Prophet* recounts the sayings of Almustafa, 'the chosen and the beloved', to the seer Almitra. His reflections on death embrace several familiar themes – the river flowing into the sea, the seeds dormant deep in the snow-clad earth, and the significance of dreams. There are echoes of the Upanishads in the remarks about breath and of Rumi in the image of standing naked in the wind and melting into the sun. But there is also a wonderful originality in the closing lines with their striking paradoxes about the possibilities that death will bring, and a powerful conviction that death can only be understood through a fuller embrace of life.

There is a particularly beautiful passage earlier in *The Prophet* which employs the familiar metaphor of setting out to sea and can, I think, be taken to express the journey from life to death. Almustafa says 'I cannot tarry longer. The sea that calls all things unto her calls me, and I must embark' and continues:

> He turned towards the sea, and saw his ship approaching the harbour, and upon her prow the mariners, the men of his own land. And his soul cried out to them, and he said: 'Sons of my ancient mother, you riders of the tides, how often have you sailed in my dreams and now you come in my awakening, which is my deeper dream. Ready am I to go, and my eagerness with sails full set awaits the wind. Only another breath will I breathe in this still air, only another loving look cast backward, and then I shall stand among you, a seafarer among seafarers.
>
> And you, vast sea, sleepless mother, who alone are peace and freedom to the river and the stream, only another winding will this stream make, only another murmur in this glade, and then shall I come to you, a boundless drop to a boundless ocean.[22]

[24] Kahlil Gibran, *The Prophet* (London: William Heinemann, 1964), p.3

Then Almitra spoke, saying, 'We would ask now of Death.'
And he said: 'You would know the secret of death.
But how shall you find it unless you seek it in the heart of life?
The owl whose night-bound eyes are blind unto the day cannot unveil
the mystery of light.
If you would indeed behold the spirit of death, open your heart wide
unto the body of life.
For life and death are one, even as the river and the sea are one.
In the depth of your hopes and desires lies your silent knowledge of the
beyond;
And like seeds dreaming beneath the snow your heart dreams of
spring.
Trust the dreams, for in them is hidden the gate to eternity.
Your fear of death is but the trembling of the shepherd when he stands
before the king whose hand is to be laid upon him in honour.
Is the shepherd not joyful beneath his trembling, that he shall wear the
mark of the king?
Yet is he not more mindful of his trembling?
For what is it to die but to stand naked in the wind and to melt into the
sun?
And what is it to cease breathing, but to free the breath from its restless
tides, that it may rise and expand and seek God unencumbered?
Only when you drink from the river of silence shall you indeed sing.
And when you have reached the mountain top, then you shall begin to
climb.
And when the earth shall claim your limbs, then shall you truly dance.'

EPILOGUE
A Safe Lodging, a Holy Rest and Peace at Last

This anthology ends as it began with a very simple prayer that may be said with someone who is dying or, indeed, at any stage of life, be it troublous or not.

Two versions appear opposite. The first is the original, which was written by John Henry Newman for the end of a sermon he preached on 19 February 1843 on the subject of 'Wisdom and Innocence' in the church of St Mary and St Nicholas, which he had built in Littlemore, near Oxford. Seven months later, on 25 September, in the same church, he preached his last sermon as an Anglican priest on 'The Parting of Friends' prior to his reception into Roman Catholic church.

The second is the version in which the prayer is usually said now. It is a particular favourite in services of Compline and I have said it many times during my twenty years as a university chaplain when taking Compline in the beautiful St Leonard's Chapel in St Andrews. It is particularly appropriate and reassuring when used in evening devotions. I have not been able to discover who introduced the phrase 'of this troublous life' or when this happened, but it does give an added poignancy.

In either form, this prayer forms an apt ending to this book. It takes us back to the theme of 'the quiet haven', in William Wordsworth's phrase, which provides its title. There has been rather more about casting off into the sea, crossing rivers and flowing like rivers out into oceans in many of the extracts, but here we return to the simple and comforting image of death as 'a safe lodging, a holy rest and peace at the last'.

Amen to that.

May He support us all the day long,
Till the shades lengthen, and the evening comes,
and the busy world is hushed,
and the fever of life is over,
and our work is done!
Then, in His mercy may he give us safe lodging,
a holy rest, and peace at last,
through Jesus Christ our Lord. Amen.

O Lord, support us all the day long of this troublous life,
until the shades lengthen, and the evening comes,
and the busy world is hushed,
and the fever of life is over,
and our work is done!
Then, Lord, in your great mercy grant us safe lodging,
a holy rest, and peace at last,
through Jesus Christ our Lord. Amen.

Sources

Prologue Prayers of commendation from the Office of Commendation in *Celebrating Common Prayer* (Mowbray, 1992) ©The European Province of the Society of St Francis 1992. Reproduced with permission.

1 Scripture quotation from the Authorised (King James) Version. Rights in the Authorised Version in the United Kingdom are vested in the Crown. Reproduced by permission of the Crown's patentee, Cambridge University Press.

2 Selected extracts from Book 4 of the Brhadaranyaka Upanishad translated from the Sanskrit for this anthology by Nicholas Ostler.

3 *The Sacred Books of the East*, Vol. XV, The Upanishads, Part II, trans. Max Muller (Oxford: The Clarendon Press, 1884), p. 41.

4 Benjamin Jowett (ed.), *The Dialogues of Plato*, Vol. II, 3rd edn. (Oxford: Oxford University Press, 1892), pp. 206–207.

5 Scripture quotations from the New Revised Standard Version Bible, copyright © 1989 the Division of Christian Education of the National Council of the Churches of Christ in the United States of America. Used by permission. All rights reserved.

6 Scripture quotation from the Authorised (King James) Version. Rights in the Authorised Version in the United Kingdom are vested in the Crown. Reproduced by permission of the Crown's patentee, Cambridge University Press.

7 Cicero, *De Senectute*, trans. Andrew Peabody (Boston: Little, Brown & Company, 1887), pp. 57, 59, 62.

8 Scripture quotations from the Revised Standard Version of the Bible, copyright © 1946, 1952 and 1971, National Council of the Churches of Christ in the United States of America. Used by permission. All rights reserved worldwide.

9 Scripture quotation from the Authorised (King James) Version. Rights in the Authorised Version in the United Kingdom are vested in the Crown. Reproduced by permission of the Crown's patentee, Cambridge University Press.

10 Scripture quotation from the Authorised (King James) Version. Rights in the Authorised Version in the United Kingdom are vested in the Crown. Reproduced by permission of the Crown's patentee, Cambridge University Press.

11 *Meditations of the Emperor Marcus Aurelius,* translated by Francis Hutcheson and James Moore (Glasgow: Robert Foulis, 1742), pp. 49, 76, 148.

12 Adamnan, *Life of St Columba*, trans. William Reeves (Edinburgh: Edmonston & Douglas, 1874), pp. 98–99.

13 *Bede's Ecclesiastical History of England*, ed. and trans. A. M. Sellar (London: George Bell, 1907), Book 2, Ch. 13, p. 117.

14 Translation by Ian Bradley from Johannis Scoti Erigenae, *De Divisione Naturae*, ed. C. B. Schlüter (Monasterii Guestphalerum, 1838), Book I, lines 515, 519, Book III, lines 683, 689.

15 *Brendaniana: Brendan the Voyager in Story and Legend*, ed. and trans. Denis Donoghue (Dublin: Browne & Nolan, 1893), pp. 112–113.

16 *Songs of Praise*, ed. Percy Dearmer (London: Oxford University Press, 1936), no. 439.

17 *Selected Poems from the Divani Shamsi Tabriz, translated by Reynold Nicholson (Cambridge: Cambridge University Press, 1898), No. XXIV, pp. 95–97; Rumi, Poet and Mystic: Selections from his Writings*, trans. Reynold Nicholson (London: George Allen & Unwin, 1950), p. 36.

18 *Rumi, Poet and Mystic: Selections from his Writings*, trans. Reynold Nicholson (London: George Allen & Unwin, 1950), pp. 109–110.

19 W. Joseph Walter, *Sir Thomas More: His Life and Times*, 2nd edn (London: Charles Dolman, 1840), p. 345; Philip Stubbes, *A Christal Glass for Christian Women* (London: T. Orin, 1592), p. 124; *The English Hymnal* (London: Oxford University Press,1933), No. 401.

20 *The Oxford Book of English Verse*, ed. Arthur Quiller-Couch (Oxford: Oxford University Press, 1919), No. 176.

21 Thomas Campion, *Two Books of Ayres* (London: Thomas Snodham, 1613), Book I, Cantus XI.

22 *The English Hymnal* (London: Oxford University Press, 1933), No. 638.

23 *The Works of John Donne*, ed. Henry Alford (London: John W. Parker, 1839), Vol. V, p. 623, Vol. 1, p. 401.

24 *The Works of George Herbert*, ed. F. E. Hutchinson (Oxford: Clarendon Press, 1941), p. 185.

25 Richard Baxter, *The Saints' Everlasting Rest* (Edinburgh: James Taylor, 1889), pp. 17, 23, 32–33, 40, 67, 76, 78.

26 *The Poems of Henry Vaughan, Silurist*, ed. E. K. Chambers, Vol. I (London: G. Routledge & Sons, 1900), p. 280.

27 *The Poems of Henry Vaughan, Silurist*, ed. E. K. Chambers, Vol. I (London: Routledge & Sons, 1900), p. 182.

28 *The Works of Mr A. Cowley in Prose and Verse*, selected by Richard Hurd, Vol. II (London: John Sharpe, 1809), pp. 203–204.

29 John Bunyan, *The Pilgrim's Progress* (London: The Folio Society, 1962), p. 147.

30 William Penn, *Some Fruits of Solitude* (London: Headley Brothers, 1905), pp. 102, 136–137.

31 *Hymns Ancient and Modern* (London: William Clowes, 1875), No. 536.

32 James Boswell, *Life of Samuel Johnson*, ed. George Hill (London: John Murray, 1835), Vol. II, pp. 476–481, 28 March 1772.

33 William Wordsworth, *Poems*, Vol.2 (London: Longman, Hurst, Rees, Orme & Brown, 1815), pp. 349–350, 354.

34 *The Works of William E. Channing* (Boston: American Unitarian Association, 1903), Vol. IV, pp. 234–236 (for earlier extracts pp. 223, 226–227, 233–234).

35 John Henry Newman, *Verses on Various Occasions* (London: Burns, Oates & Co., 1868), p. 206.

36 Christina Rossetti, *Poems* (Boston: Little, Brown & Co., 1906), p. 24.

37 Christina Rossetti, *Poems* (Boston: Little, Brown & Co., 1906), p. 93.

38 *Hymns Ancient and Modern* (London: William Clowes, 1875), No. 608.

39 *The Poems of Adelaide Anne Procter* (New York: Hurst & Company,1858), p. 69.

40 Adelaide Anne Procter, *Legends and Lyrics* (London: George Bell, 1892), pp. 149–150.

41 *Poems of Arthur Hugh Clough* (London: Macmillan, 1920), p. 196.

42 F. D. Maurice, *Lectures on the Apocalypse*, 3rd edn (London: Macmillan & Co., 1893), pp. 64–65.

43 *An American Anthology*, ed. Edmund Stedman (Boston: Houghton Mifflin, 1900), No. 645.

44 *Happy Voices: New Hymns and Tunes* (New York: American Tract Society, 1865), No. 220.

45 *The Dream of Gerontius by John Henry Cardinal Newman* (London: Burns & Oates, 1865), pp. 33–36.

46 *The Poetical Works of John Greenleaf Whittier*, Vol. II (Boston: Houghton Mifflin & Co., 1892), p. 267.

47 Christina Rossetti, *Poems* (Boston: Little, Brown & Co., 1906), Part 2, pp. 122, 31; Christina Rossetti, *The Face of the Deep: A Devotional Commentary on the Apocalypse* (London: SPCK, 1893), p. 144.

48 *Church Hymns with Tunes* (London: SPCK, 1919), No. 247.

49 Alexander Carmichael, *Carmina Gadelica* (Edinburgh: Oliver & Boyd, 1940), p. 383.

50 J. B. T. Marsh, *The Story of the Jubilee Singers: With Their Songs* (London: Hodder & Stoughton, 1877), Nos 77, 89.

51 William Ernest Henley, *Poems* (London: David Nutt, 1919), p. 110.

52 Christina Rossetti, *Poems* (Boston: Little, Brown & Co., 1906), p. 130

53 *The Church Hymnary* (Edinburgh: Henry Frowde, 1901), No. 207.

54 George Matheson, *Moments on the Mount* (New York: A. C. Armstrong, 1884), pp. 182–183.

55 *The Complete Poems of Alfred, Lord Tennyson* (New York, Frederick A. Stokes, 1891, p. 464.

56 *The Complete Savoy Operas*, Vol.II (London: The Folio Society, 1994), p. 178.

57 Benjamin Jowett (ed.), *The Dialogues of Plato*, Vol. II, 3rd edn (London: Oxford University Press, 1892), pp.180–182.

58 George Matheson, *Searchings in the Silence* (London: Cassell, 1895), pp. 210–212.

59 George Matheson, *Rests by the River* (New York: A. C. Armstrong, 1906), pp. 27–28.

60 Kahlil Gibran, *The Prophet* (London: William Heinemann, 1964), pp. 93–94.

Epilogue John Henry Newman, *Sermons Bearing on the Subjects of the Day* (London: Rivingtons, 1869), p. 307.